ANNUAL SHOWCASE

Reflections And Reverie

Edited By Andy Porter

First published in Great Britain in 2024 by:

Young Writers
Remus House
Coltsfoot Drive
Peterborough
PE2 9BF
Telephone: 01733 890066
Website: www.youngwriters.co.uk

All Rights Reserved
Book Design by Ashley Janson
© Copyright Contributors 2024
Softback ISBN 978-1-83685-018-2
Printed and bound in the UK by BookPrintingUK
Website: www.bookprintinguk.com
YB0619B

Foreword

Since 1991, here at Young Writers we have celebrated the awesome power of creative writing, especially in children and young adults where it can serve as a vital method of expressing their emotions and views about the world around them.

Usually our creative writing competitions focus on either fiction or poetry in all its forms, but that does leave a gap for other writing skills and styles to fall through. What about all the writing that doesn't fit into either of those categories? Songs and scripts, blogs and book reviews, essays and articles; we wanted to read and celebrate those too! So we created the Annual Showcase, a competition where any style of writing could be submitted up to 1000 words.

Open to all 4-18 year-olds, the Annual Showcase was the perfect opportunity for any budding young writer, or their proud parent or teacher, to submit a piece of writing on any topic and in any style. The extended word limit also allowed these authors to write at length, really exploring their ideas and imagination.

All the entries we've received have been a delight to read. On every topic conceivable, in every style, they prove that these young writers are bursting with ideas and creativity; we just need to give them an outlet! We really hope we've done that with the Annual Showcase, and we hope that you enjoy reading them as much as we have!

Contents

Independent Entrants

Alice Psichockaite (9)	1
Rihana Prilogan (11)	2
Hope Miles (9)	7
Lucas Cesariny Tremblay Monteiro (11)	8
Hafsa Rawfy (11)	13
Aabrita Khan (10)	14
Isla Smith (10)	18
Sophie Robertshaw (10)	22
Kaya Odedra (12)	26
Jade Buckley (11)	30
Nia Roberts (10)	34
Grace Green (11)	38
Sophia Jacobs (11)	42
Eva Bryant (10)	46
Muhammad Arfeen Fazal (10)	50
Senuka Fernando (10)	54
Neha Sathiyamoorthy (9)	58
Sacha Imankerdjo Lambert (11)	62
Mohamed Mahamed (11)	65
Darcy Bickford-Kehoe (10)	66
Alexander Ivanov (9)	69
Christopher O'Dornan (11)	70
Wren Jervis-McNamara (6)	73
Abigail O'Dornan (9)	74
George James Smith (9)	77
Jasmine Carbaugh (11)	78
Dilys Hall	81
Isata Kamara (9)	82
Ben Dinh (9)	85
Joycie Arcos (10)	86
Mehdi-Ali Shah	89
Fidelity Matthew (9)	90
Nikola Ivanov (8)	93
Athena Pointon (11)	94
Amna Athar (11)	96
Saanvi Upadhyaya (11)	98
Jasmine Cumberbatch (7)	100
Saanvi Bolisetty (11)	102
Sidney Nicholson (10)	104
Luna Stevens (11)	106
Siya Bisht (9)	109
Aalisha Tyagi (11)	110
Akshayan Vivekanantharajah (8)	112
Jacob Rawlinson (10)	114
Lexi Warrington (9)	116
Lena Saif (8)	118
Athena Smith (11)	120
Yatharth Rangineni (12)	122
Evaline Lewak (8)	124
Annabel Grace Woods (10)	126
Aoife Attwood (10)	128
Mia James (8)	130
Isla Tully (10)	132
Raeesah Khan (11)	134
Sanvi Patel (10)	136
Katherine O'Dornan (9)	138
Kevin Kovacs (8)	140
Joseph Lewin (6)	142
Esha Raheel (11)	143
Hussain Atif Lone (10)	144
Danielle Erikume (11)	145
Harnek Landa (8)	146
Imogen Lewis (7)	147
Noella Cobbinah (8)	148
Dillon Clarke (10)	149
Casey O'Rourke (10)	150
Levi Pitts (9)	151
Nancy Rossiter-Pointer (11)	152

Khadija Azeem (6)	153
Miri Fogel (10)	154
Grace Merle McGuire (4)	155
Eva Udy (10)	156
Louise Lin (11)	157
Muhammad Hunnain Ali Shah (11)	158
Amyra Qoudos (8)	159
Emily Rose Hopewell (8)	160
Stuti Shah (10)	161
Ali Abdullah (9)	162
Annalisa Burton (12)	163
Harmony James (4)	164
Summer Grainger (10)	165
Ozichukwu Egbeogu (5)	166
Kerem Dogan (7)	167
Josie Pollard (10)	168
Thananiya Thevakanthan (9)	169
Eshaal Fatima Shah	170
Aanya Kaul (5)	171
Spencer Brookes (11)	172

THE CREATIVE WRITING

Besties Kivi And Little Star

Somewhere up there, high in the sky, there lived a little star. And there, down on the ground, lived a kitty named 'Kivi'. She was called Kivi because she had green eyes, similar to a kiwi.

Every night, the kitty Kivi sat comfortably on the windowsill and looked high into the sky. And then one day Kivi saw a small star in the sky, which was shining so brightly and illuminated the entire window and the windowsill on which the kitty cat was lying. So they met, the little bright star and the kitty Kivi. And now, as soon as night fell, the kitty hurried on the windowsill and with her green eyes she was looking for a small bright star in the sky. And there, high in the sky, a little star was impatiently waiting for the darkness to appear in the sky and shine brightly for her new and best friend, the kitty Kivi.

Both friends, the star and the kitty were happy to meet every night and looked forward to the darkness. And then the next night the little star, as always, was in a hurry to please and surprise her best friend Kivi and appeared in her place earlier than usual. She really wanted to surprise Kivi and shine in the sky for her even brighter, but the little star tried so hard that it burned out and its bright light did not reach the ground... and the kitty Kivi no longer saw the light of her little star.

But still, the kitty Kivi comes to the window every night and looks in the sky with her green eyes for her little best friend an asterisk, and a little star appears in the sky every night and shines for her kitty Kivi, although her light is no longer so bright and is not visible on Earth. This is such a devoted friendship between Kivi and the little star.

Alice Psichockaite (9)

Carla And The Bag Surprise!

In a huge, modern city, the summer holidays were over and school was about to start. Every child loved getting new stationery and a bag, especially from a shop called 'Back To School Needs'. Inside, it was crowded with lots of children, mainly around the superhero bag section. Not only that, but a hamster was also hiding in a corner of the shop. Jumping as quickly as possible, the tiny hamster moved inside a bag. *Ding!* A beautiful, tall, and joyful girl walked into the shop.
"Hey there, Carla! What are you doing?" said Mrs Worthington, the shop owner.
"Just came to grab a bag!" Carla replied while looking around.
"Okay, just so you know, you may want to check out the superhero bag section," the shop owner suggested.
"Nah, it's fine. I'll just grab this one," she answered, holding up a bag. The bag was huge, with lots of pockets. Carla walked toward the till and handed Mrs Worthington the bag she wanted.
"Are you sure that's the only item you want?" Worthington questioned her.
"Yep!" Carla responded, giving her the money.
"Bye!" Mrs Worthington exclaimed happily.
"Bye!" the girl replied as she ran quickly toward home.
"Hi, Mum!" she shouted upon entering.
"Hi, Carla! That bag looks really nice," her mum replied.

Carla dashed upstairs into her room. While changing out of her clothes, she heard a noise. *Wow! What was that?!* she thought.

Gently, Carla opened her bag, noticing there was a hamster inside.

"Hi... um! Who are you? What are you doing in my bag?" she exclaimed.

"Uh! I'm... I... I'm sorry; I didn't mean to," said the hamster quietly.

"Wait, you can talk!" Carla shouted.

"Is everything alright there?" her mum called.

"Yep, Mum!" she replied, feeling confused.

"Okay, so you can talk?" Carla asked the hamster.

"Yeah..." the animal replied.

"What is your name?" Carla asked, surprised.

"Harriet," it answered.

"Okay, so you're a hamster who can talk, named Harriet?" Carla said.

"Duh!" Harriet replied.

"Look, Harriet, do you want to be my pet for now?" she asked.

"Sure!" Harriet responded cheerfully.

The sun rose, and it was the first day of Year Six for Carla. She had dreamt all night about her pet making mischief at school. Oh no, she was about to be late again! Once she arrived, Carla could see everyone getting ready for their first lesson, including Lexi. Lexi always hated Carla and was rude to her. Carla noticed an opportunity for revenge.

Carla ran up behind Lexi without noticing. She grabbed her hamster out of her bag and placed it in front of her.
"Hi, Carla! How was your holiday? Ugly, right? Ha ha!" shouted Lexi.
"Shut up!" Carla exclaimed.
"It's okay; I know what to do!" said Lexi, walking away.
Suddenly, Lexi tripped over the hamster. Quickly, Carla put Harriet back in her bag, and everyone laughed at Lexi.
When Carla arrived in her first lesson, everyone wanted to talk to her.
"That was cool, Carla!" said a boy.
"I was about to cry because of how funny it was!" said Carla's best friend.
"Thanks! It's not just me; it's also Harriet, my hamster!" replied Carla, grabbing Harriet.
"Hi!" exclaimed Harriet.
"OMG, he's adorable!" said a girl happily.
"He talks?!?" shouted another person.
"Yeah!" Carla answered.
"That's cool!" said a guy.
"I know, right?!" shouted another.
Then, the headteacher interrupted their conversation.
"Can I have Carla, please?" he called.
"Oh, okay, I've got to go," Carla whispered to her friends.
While Carla was in his office, her friends listened in.
"I've heard, Mrs Carla, that you brought a pet to school," the headteacher said politely.
"Who told you that?!?" questioned Carla.

"Lexi Bonners, but I haven't called you for bad news; it's good news!" he replied.

"What is it?!" Carla screamed back.

"You are selected to go with your pet hamster to the 'Best Pet of All Schools' competition!" Mr Emanuel said happily.

"Yay!" screamed all her friends from outside.

"What was that?" questioned the headteacher.

"Nothing... but what day is it?" Carla asked.

"Tomorrow, so you need to be ready!" he said.

"Okay, bye!" Carla exclaimed while leaving. Her friends lifted her up in the air until they reached class.

The bell rang at the end of school. Carla arrived home ready to share the news.

"Hi, Mum! I got selected to go to a competition tomorrow!" shouted Carla.

"Sounds like you'll have a fun day tomorrow!" replied her mum.

Carla went to her room and thought about what to wear for herself and Harriet the next day.

The sun rose, and it was the day of the competition. Harriet and Carla both dressed in matching outfits and ran to the event. It was crowded with representatives. Carla could not wait to see what would happen and who would win. Around her, she saw cute outfits, but none were better than theirs. Carla and Harriet set up the place, ready for their turn. Everyone was ready, and it was their time to shine. After many others had their turns, it was finally Carla and Harriet's turn.

"Hi there! I'm Carla, and this is my hamster, Harriet! We have matching outfits!" said Carla.

"Hello! I can talk!" Harriet added.
Every representative was shocked at the talking hamster.
Later, the judges announced the winners.
"Okay, we have decided the winners!" exclaimed the judges.
"It's... Carla and Harriet from Ealing Primary School!"
Cheers erupted as Carla and Harriet held the trophy.
Once they returned to school, everyone was excited about their win. A new trophy was placed in the school display.
"Well done, Carla!" said her best friend.
"I knew you could do it!" said another.
"It was very nice for you and your pet to represent our school," said Mr Emanuel.
Everyone was so proud of her.

Rihana Prilogan (11)

Axol The Protector

Once upon a time, there was a very beautiful, smart phoenix named Axol. He was flying through the forest one evening when he came across an elder magician who needed his help. The phoenix would become a protector of the land. The phoenix thought on this and knew it was what he was born to do. The magician explained he would need to become a tattoo on the prince of the land when he was not needed but he would live forever and he would transfer to the prince's son when he came of age. The phoenix quickly agreed.
So for many years, the phoenix would come alive when he was needed to protect the land and his people from all dangers. Then one day a large sea creature came to shore ready to battle and kill everyone in the village. The phoenix was ready to battle to death to save his people.
It was a hard battle and there was great loss to both sides. The sea monster was killed, but also killed Axol the phoenix too. The village was joyous but also the grief of losing their beloved protector was so much they burnt their bodies in a burial.
Once they were settled around the fire and the village was going to sleep, only a few villagers stayed behind when all of a sudden there was a burst of great light out of the ashes of Axol the great protector. Everyone cried with joy, he was returned to them. Not only was he a protector but their loyal friend.
Axol lived for eternity and always looked after his village and the people in it.

Hope Miles (9)

Good Versus Crime: Super Squad Versus The Vicious Five

One day, a group of friends were playing in the park and were excited for the weekend Gala day. You might be asking how this related to good vs crime, but soon you will know. This group of friends was not as normal as you think because they called themselves the Super Squad. The Super Squad has four members: Dogman, Stink, Roboboy, and Skye. Hidden within the city, these four extraordinary individuals always upheld justice. Together, they had a unique and common purpose: to protect their city and the innocent from the bad guys.
"It's Saturday! Happy Gala Day!" shouted out Dogman when he woke up. But then his super buzzer started to make a noise and that meant something was happening in the city.
"Not today," said Dogman while he called the rest of the Super Squad and asked them to go to the HQ as soon as possible because something had happened in the city.
After everyone arrived at HQ, they looked at the big screen to see what was happening. On the screen, it said that the Diamond of Space had disappeared.
"Check the CCTV footage from last night, Dogman?" Skye asked.
"Okay," Dogman replied. Dogman turned on the CCTV camera, but nothing happened until... Roboboy saw a figure sneaking passed security.

"Look, it's Doomer, the leader of the Vicious Five!" Roboboy shouted.
"It is! And he's trying to steal the diamond," Stink said.
"Those creepy monsters again!" whispered Dogman.
"But where's the rest of his group?" Skye asked. Dogman switched the camera.
"Look at that big purple van," Roboboy said.
"Did you say a big purple van?" Dogman asked.
"Yeah, why?" Roboboy replied.
"There's only one family in town who owns a big purple van," Dogman said, trying to keep his tears from flowing like a river.
"Whose family?" Stink asked.
"Mine," Dogman replied sadly. "But this doesn't make any sense," Dogman said, confused.
"But it could," Skye said gently.
"How!" Dogman shouted.
"How often have we been to your house for a sleepover?" Skye asked.
"Ten times, so," Dogman replied.
"So out of those ten, how many times have your parents left before we went to bed?" Skye asked.
"Ten times," Dogman answered, realising what'd been happening.
"And every single time something was happening when they were gone," Skye said.
"This all makes sense now. My parents are part of the Vicious Five and didn't want to tell me because they know I'm part of the Super Squad and I would get them arrested, but we're not 100% sure," Dogman said.

"Look, Doomer's going inside your parents' van, and the rest of his group is inside," Stink said.

"My parents are innocent," said Dogman.

"I have a plan," Skye said.

"The plan is Stink and I will stay here to check all the cameras in town and tell Dogman and Roboboy on walkie-talkies where to go. Got it?" Skye shouted.

So, then Skye and Stink turned on every camera in town and Dogman and Roboboy were waiting for their instructions.

"They're passing by our school," Skye said.

"Okay," Dogman replied.

"Now they're passing by the shops," Skye said.

"We're on our way there," Roboboy responded.

"Now they stopped," Stink said quietly.

"Where?" Dogman asked.

"At your house," Stink replied.

"What!" Dogman said in shock.

"Don't worry, we'll be there to help," Stink said.

A few minutes later, Stink and Skye arrived at Dogman's house. They went inside to check if anyone was there, but no one was inside. They checked every single room but couldn't find anyone.

"Let's check the basement," Roboboy suggested.

"No!" Dogman shouted.

"Why? What's the problem?" Stink asked.

"My parents forbid me from going in there," Dogman responded loudly.

"But that's the only place they could be, plus if we find out the truth, we can make them and the Vicious Five good," Skye said.

"Okay, let's go," Dogman said nervously.
So, the Super Squad walked down into the basement quietly so if the Vicious Five were in, they would not hear them.
"It sounds like people are talking. Let's see what it is!" Stink shouted. Someone walked down the stairs. "Quick, hide behind the shelf," Dogman said. But when the people came down to the basement, Dogman could not hold his feelings and shouted, "Mum, Dad, what is going on?"
"Be quiet, son!" Dogman's parents shouted.
"Mum, Dad, this isn't like you?" Dogman said.
"This is what happened," said a voice in the shadows.
Zzz!
"W-w-what happened?" Dogman asked.
"We got tazed, Dogman," Roboboy said.
"Well, well, well, I see that you've finally woken up," Doomer said with a creepy smile.
"What have you done to my parents?!" Dogman shouted.
"Nothing, just a bit of mind control," Doomer said casually.
"Where are they?" Dogman asked.
"I can't tell you," replied Doomer. Dogman was so angry he tried to run away until... *Bang!*
"What's this?" Dogman asked.
"It's my invisible cage. Well, it's time for me to plan another heist, adios amigos," Doomer replied.
"Let us out of here!" Dogman shouted.
"Don't worry, Dogman," Stink said.
Stink used his tech genius, so he manipulated electricity and hacked Doomer's system to easily turn the enemy's technology against them.

"Let's show them who we are," Dogman said.

With his parents now controlled by Stink, the Super Squad combined their powers and quickly defeated the Vicious Five and Dogman removed the control button from his parents so they couldn't be controlled again. Now they were back to normal and hugged him with all their might.

With the Vicious Five defeated and the diamond returned to Space City, the Super Squad stood victorious. But they knew their work was far from over as they needed to control the city for the Gala Day Festival.

"Happy Gala Day everyone!" shouted the Super Squad.

The Super Squad had become a symbol of justice and heroes.

Lucas Cesariny Tremblay Monteiro (11)

A Letter

To whom it may concern,

I am writing to express my ongoing concerns about the violence in Gaza, which has an impact on many citizens. Did you know that over 28,000 Palestinians have been killed, while thousands remain missing under the residue of destroyed buildings?

More than 200 days of war have taken an unimaginable toll on children in the Gaza Strip. Over 15,000 children have died and over 12,000 have been wounded: 20,000 were missing. In October, families were given no choice but to evacuate and to take shelter in Rafah, 250,000 to 1.2 million. Can you believe they are treating us this way? This is outrageous, they are literally treating us like animals. Do you think we deserve to be treated like that? Or should we be treated better?

I think you should think and act fast and help all these generous, innocent and helpful people that people may think are scumbags. They are literally doing nothing and they are still getting punished and all you do is sit around and drink a cup of tea and do nothing to help the innocent but just helping the bad. These things are still going on so you can still act now. Helping with everything that is all in a mess in Gaza will help very much. It would improve Gaza and your kindness.

Yours sincerely,
Hafsa.

Hafsa Rawfy (11)

Escaping The Workhouse

The acrid streets were infested with rodents and grime. The gutters were decorated with muck and dirt from the hooves of horses. A foul stench seeped out of the houses as urchins trembled under newspapers, huddling together for warmth. Yet amidst this urban misery, there lay a place even more wretched - a place that made the streets seem like a mere prelude. It was the workhouse.

The building's exterior was a patchwork of crumbling infrastructure. Decades of rain and neglect had etched lines into its surface, like wrinkles on an elderly man's face. The colossal walls loomed over anyone who dared to stare at it. They seemed to lean inward as if conspiring to keep the world out. The entrance was a squat gatehouse flanked by two stone lions: their once fierce expressions now worn down. Around the workhouse, the air seemed to be laden with the ghosts of broken souls. Its walls absorbed the cries of the downtrodden, echoing them.

Behind the unyielding iron bars of the workhouse gates, a multitude of people languished - a sea of sullen faces revealing the fear that had taken root within. The miserable, feeble people - once hopeful, now broken - had arrived seeking refuge. They carried stories of loss, of hunger, of dreams crushed like leaves underfoot.

Within the cold, shadowed corridors of the workhouse, another horror lurked within - the Master held sway - a spider at the centre of its web. His eyes, sharp as shards of glass, swept over the huddled forms before him - the very souls meant to find solace within these walls. And yet, there he stood, a mockery of compassion. The air thickened as he surveyed the destitute faces - their cheeks hollow, their eyes like extinguished stars.

Yet in the oppressive gloom, two indomitable souls conspired - night after night, week after week - to defy the cruel fate that loomed over them. Two children, abruptly thrust from one world into another, now found themselves confined within the austere walls of a place known only as the 'cage of torment.' After meticulous effort, their cunning plan had finally coalesced.

Emily and Elijah, bound by blood as siblings.

Emily, at the age of ten, possessed hair as dark as the moonless night sky. Her emerald eyes sparkled in the sunlight, indicating a concealed inferno within. From the very moment she and her brother were cast into the unforgiving embrace of the workhouse, Emily's determination blazed like a solitary star against the gloom. She was not merely fierce; she was a tempest - a force to be reckoned with. Her intelligence, sharp as a shard of glass, fuelled her audacity. Yet, for all her daring, there lingered an impulsive streak-a willingness to leap before looking.

At eight years old, Elijah stood on the cusp of childhood, his innocence still intact. His hair, a cascade of sunlit strands, seemed to capture the very essence of golden mornings. His eyes - deep, brown pools - held stories untold. They were the colour of ancient oak bark, reflecting both the weight of the world and the promise of better days. Unlike his impulsive sister, he navigated life with deliberate steps. Anger rarely found a foothold in his heart; instead, kindness surged from him like a gentle stream. When others stumbled, he offered a steady hand, as if born to be a refuge for weary souls. His mind, a compass, pointed toward safety and strategy. Calculated moves, not impetuous leaps, guided him - a rarity in this world.

Emily and Elijah, their hearts drumming a wild rhythm, slipped from their beds like smoke through cracks. The moon, their silent accomplice, spilt silver across the room. Their breaths - held hostage by anticipation - barely escaped their lips. Elijah's eyes met Emily's, and without words, they understood tonight was their reckoning. The workhouse, that pit of despair, would no longer shackle them. They were shadows with purpose, ghosts of defiance. The window beckoned - a portal to the unknown. Emily's fingers found a forgotten straw, brittle as their dreams. She wove the Devil's Tongue Knot, binding hope and desperation. The rope dangled - a lifeline spun from threads of rebellion.

And then - the room crackled. The floorboards groaned, protesting their audacity. The staff, alerted by fate or spite, surged forward.

"Grab the rope, fools!" Matron's voice, dripping disdain, echoed like a curse. But Emily held on. Her knuckles blanched, veins singing with determination. She wouldn't surrender this fragile chance - not to bullies, not to fate. Elijah's whisper cut through the chaos: "What is that?"

"It's *the other kids!*" Emily's defiance rose from tremor to battle cry. Those who shared their misery, their dreams, surged forward. The rope strained, a bridge between desperation and freedom.

"We're with you, Elijah and Emily!" The chorus swelled - a symphony of rebellion. Their footsteps, once muffled by oppression, now thundered. The children - no longer just victims - pulled with ferocity. The rope threatened to snap, but they held on, teeth gritted, eyes aflame.

Outside, the moonlit forest awaited, though miles away - a sanctuary of secrets. Emily's pulse raced. She imagined dew-kissed grass underfoot, the scent of pine, and the taste of freedom. Elijah's grip tightened. They weren't alone; they were part of something larger - a fragile alliance born of desperation and anguish.

And then - the rope gave way. The adults fell, defeated. The children spilt through the angelic doorway - their escape etched in moonbeams. They were free. Forever. Emily glanced back at the workhouse, its oppressive walls fading into memory. The tattered portrait of a forgotten matron seemed to wink. Had she, too, once whispered defiance into the night? Emily nodded slightly at her, as if sending her a silent message and then followed the band of children.

As they sprinted into the forest, Emily and Elijah vowed: they wouldn't just survive; they'd thrive. Their footsteps left imprints - the path to a new dawn. And the Devil's Tongue Knot, still snug in Emily's palm, whispered promises of justice and a new beginning for her and her friends.

Aabrita Khan (10)

The Cornfield

As the moon rose and the sun set, a scarecrow-like figure roamed the unexplored depths of a large cornfield. The shadowy being was as tall as a grand oak rooted into the ground. Every night when wolves howl on a full moon, this strange presence appears from nowhere. Several children have nightmares after hearing about this horrific and terrifying legend roaming the field...
"Fine mum! I'll be in bed by 10pm."
"And your sister, Karry?" asked my mother.
"9pm. I know," I replied.
Once my mum and dad left, it was just my sister and I with our dog Loki. I made extra cheesy mac and cheese from a box. It was delicious; however, my sister didn't think so as she gave it to the dog instead! For dessert, we had banoffee pie and Karry ate it all. She had three big spoonfuls and all I was left with was the crumbs!
"Get ready for bed Karry. It's already 8:45!" I exclaimed, whilst washing the dishes.
"No!" bellowed Karry as she stamped her foot. With a grin, she then ran upstairs to the attic and hid from me. I dashed upstairs as quickly as I could to find her giggling behind a pile of brown boxes. Once I found her, I dragged her to her room whilst kicking and screaming.
"Come on! It's already 9:05pm, I was meant to put you to bed five minutes ago!" I shouted.
"Fine!" screamed my annoying little sister, crossing her arms.

Once she was ready, I put her to bed and turned the lights off. I went into the living room and watched a little more TV, before getting ready for bed. I wanted an early night so I could be fresh and fully awake for my daily jog in the morning.

I woke to a sudden thud. It was still dark. I looked outside my window but I saw nothing. I decided to have a quick look outside. There was nothing. I turned around and the door was shut. I couldn't open it. It was locked and I didn't have my keys. I tried all the windows but... they were locked. Continuously, I banged the door as hard as I could, calling my sister's name, hoping she was awake. "Karry, Karry!" I screamed but it was no use, she didn't answer. I took a deep breath considering what to do next.

The wind began to pick up. I shivered as a powerful gust struck my face, leaving me feeling even more anxious about being stuck outside at this time of night.

Another cold blast of wind hit me. However, this time, I was sure I heard my name hurrying past me through the night sky. Then, there it was again, the muffled murmur of my name moving slowly in the direction of the cornfield. Caught up in curiosity, my heart began to race with intrigue. I started to follow the sound of my name being whispered in the air.

There was a glow which seemed to be coming from a maze of cornstalks. As I got closer, the cornstalks got taller and fuller. The maze began to engulf me but despite the fear of potentially getting lost, I knew the light was guiding me to something incredible.

The wind began to drop and as I looked up at the sky, the dark clouds parted revealing a full moon. As the rest of the town slept, nature awakened. In the distance I vaguely heard the echo of mountain wolves howling, the night owls hooting, and the hidden crickets chirping. There it was again! My name. My attention got drawn back to the glowing light through the corn, which now felt like it was right in front of me.

Walking into the depths of the cornfield, the mysterious voice got louder and louder. Finally, I saw the shape of a large figure. It looked like a scarecrow; however, the shadowy body was moving awkwardly and with difficulty, but definitely moving. Panicked, I recalled the legend that all the town kids knew about the cornfields:

'Every night when a wolf howls on a full moon a strange body appears from nowhere. If you are one of the unfortunate ones to encounter him, your dreams will be doomed forever!'

We always thought it was a scary tale to make children go to sleep, but now I was not so sure.

I stood frozen with fear as he got closer. Its head jerked forward as his beady eyes stared right into my soul. With desperation, my mind raced trying to remember the rest of the legend in hope there was some advice; I was sure there was! I stepped back as he advanced further towards me. He reached out his straw-like arm as if he was about to grab me. The way he pointed triggered something in my mind. "That's it!" I cried. "To save your dreams you must point at this spirit and chant 'come dawn, bring the day and take him away!'"

With courage and determination, I found my voice and started to chant. To my surprise, the scarecrow-like figure began to falter. I chanted it again, and this time I raised my arm and pointed my quivering finger at him. He seemed to back away, and at the same time, the first glimpse of sunlight crept into the distance. I felt a surge of hope in my heart; it worked! The dawn was coming to save me! Repeatedly, I chanted until the sun had risen and he stood frozen like a lifeless scarecrow in the cornfield once more. Relieved, I turned around and ran back towards my home. Mum and Dad's car was back in the driveway, and thankfully there was no panic coming from the house. They must have gone straight to bed last night thinking I was soundly sleeping in my room. I took a deep breath in preparation for the worst telling-off I was about to get; this could be scarier than the walking scarecrow! I knocked on the door and waited.

A sleepy dad opened the front door.

"Been out for your jog already?" yawned Dad.

"Yeah, that's right," I muttered in shock.

I had got away with it!

With relief, I stepped through the front door, briefly taking a second to look back at the sunlit path that led to the cornfield.

Isla Smith (10)

The Inner Workings Of Sophie's Head

Hello there! This is *the best story* ever, your mind will be blown by what you read *and it will sound like this. Boom!* Is your mind blown yet? *It is, don't lie. Do you like this book? You do, don't lie!*
Things about me!....
I like playing Roblox.
I *hate* being bored.
I love cats, I love Donovan (my cat).
I like using CAPITAL LETTERS.
We'll start at Year 2.

Year Two:
I thought I liked the teacher in Year Two (*I put toe instead of two, haha!*). Well, she was strict, but she played music in any free time we had. Some people would say she was the best (*no*, I'm the best). I'm not really sure what to write. Oh, in that year (2020) it snowed so much I got out of maths. I'm a little *dum*, see I spelt *dumb wrong.*
In Year 2 it was *lockdown* and I was happy I got out of maths many times! Mum and Dad had to work, so I FaceTimed my grandparents and did work with them over the phone. I didn't have Roblox back then, I had Minecraft and I was good in creative but not survival. I could go on for ages but you don't want to sit here for 5 years.
I watched stuff on the TV and ate and slept in lots... *And that's all for today people.* I hope this book makes me rich, a nine-year-old million *billion trillionaire*, sounds good, doesn't it?

Year Three:
Yes, so in Year 3 I didn't *know* I was *dyslexic*. Wow, I spelt '*dyslexic*' right with no spell check. The teacher would tell me off again and again, so rude, but not like a proper telling-off. Once she wanted me to redo *all* my maths work and half of my class had to stay in at break time once, and all we did was climb on a wall.

In our school we have this thing on a Friday where we have a part before home time called *golden time* and it is basically *free time* (*freedom!*). Because I went out with a teacher for help and didn't *quite* finish *all* my work, she took it out of my free time which was mean. The teaching assistant though could do amazing cartwheels, so good! The other teaching assistant had to go to Year 6 halfway through the year, he was one of the best and so, so, so much fun.

Before Year 4, a teacher did a *long* speech because she was going to teach us when our main teacher was off. This is what I remember: "I can't wait to teach you... *Blah, blah, blah.* Something about spreading our wings into learning." I don't have *wings so I can't spread them and I don't want to spread my wings on toast.* I prefer peanut butter, where *did* toast come from? *Me, stupid?* (That's me talking to myself.) Okay, *now that's it* for today.

Year Four:
I think Year 4 was one of the best school years ever because I had the best teacher ever and it was when I found out I was *dyslexic, dun, dun, dun!* So on the first day of Year 4 *I got out of spelling* so I went to a different school for an assessment and a lady asked me to do lots of stuff.

In case you didn't know, *dyslexia* is a learning disability and it turns out *I was dyslexic* and it was a really good year. *Hahaha, got you! Laugh or else.*

In Year 4 we had a residential. It was *going to be for two nights but they changed it to four nights!* Is your mind blown? It is, don't *lie.* I was in a room of five girls. And there were contests. Okay, we didn't win the tidying award (we were very messy) but we won the bin bag and toilet paper fashion competition. Bushcraft was fun roasting marshmallows (not Roblox roasting). One of my friends set their marshmallow on fire a bit! It was all melted and really warm.

The night walk was *um...* some of the children that went on it would say it was scary but *I liked it and the night line was the best.* First, before the muddy obstacle course there was the clean one which was fun then the muddy one and we put on army print jumpsuits over our clothes and it was really muddy. I went through a tunnel and... it had a massive *puddle* and my friend was saying *llamacorn in her sleep!* And somehow we were always partnered together and stabbing pencils into our knees. *Okay, that's it for Year 4.*

Year Five (Now):

So in Year 5 or now, well, I'm talking about the beginning of the year, I had three teachers. Teacher One would take minutes off break for losing a piece of equipment like a green pen (yes, she's the same teacher I had in Year Three) so I had Miss Second Teacher. She was one of the best and at Christmas, she read 'The Grumpus' to us and it's the best Christmas story ever. The best stories ever are 'Demon Dinner Lady' or any other Pamela Butchart and '*Mr Gum*'.

24

So anyway she stopped teaching us and we got Miss Third Teacher. She is good as well but she also started taking minutes off break as well. *My brain right when she said she will take minutes off for getting four or less spellings correct, nooooooo! But* she is still one of the best teachers because she lets us do fun things. Yes, *I'm* surprised my head didn't explode in Year 5.
Oh, I have a school trip in June to *Tropical World,* it's like a *zoo in my house with my sister in it anyway.* Go away now, it's the end, bye.
By the time you read this, I'm in Year 6 unless you read it in the year 2099! Thank you for wasting your time reading my long book, *bye bye! I hope it makes me rich!*

Sophie Robertshaw (10)

The Deal With The Devil

Waking up at 5am on your birthday isn't ideal. Especially when in a few hours, the whole kingdom will be watching your every move, as the new queen of Cameridia. Seamstresses poked at my rose-coloured gown as my maids fiddled with makeup brushes and fussed over my wet, brown hair. I didn't realise how hungry I was until my stomach started rumbling. Ugh, I started to regret not sneaking down to the kitchens for a pastry. As if on cue, my little sister, Avery, sauntered in with a plate of fruit and pastries.
"You are a lifesaver, Aves," I said gratefully, as I popped a green grape into my mouth, savouring the sour flavour.
"Can't have you starving on your big day!" she said. She seemed much more excited than I was. Her chestnut hair was pinned back, cascading down her back. She was wearing a royal blue coloured gown which reached the floor. Avery looked more and more like me every day.
Just as I was about to reach for another grape, the window shattered. Shards of glass flew across my bedroom, one slicing my left cheek. About thirty people, dressed in black head to toe, marched in, knives in hands.
I turned towards where Avery stood, my hands shaking, signalling for her to escape while she could. Suddenly rough hands pinned my wrists behind my back and forced me to the ground. No, no, no, not today. I tried wrenching my arms from his grip, but they wouldn't budge. My heartbeat sped up, my hands still shaking madly. Had Avery escaped? Had she gone to get the guards? Why weren't these people talking? I felt a sharp pain in my arm and then my vision went black.

My eyelids fluttered open, my vision hazy. My head was spinning, but I could figure out that I wasn't at the palace anymore. Once my vision cleared up, I stood up. Well, tried to at least. As soon as I put weight on my legs, my knees gave way, causing me to collapse on the cold, hard ground underneath me. Where was I? Metal bars surrounded me. *A dungeon. Great. I've been kidnapped. But why?*

At that moment, three men walked in, this time they weren't dressed in full black. The first man was massive. Seven feet tall was my guess. Very broad. He had a large scar running down his right eye. The second man was smaller than the first but still larger than me. *I swear I recognise him.* He had dark brown hair, slightly darker than mine and tanned skin. His eyes were a chocolate brown colour.

He seemed quite intimidating. The third man looked like the second man, but older. The second man looked older than me but probably only about two years.

"Princess Ivy of Cameridia, what a pleasure to finally meet you," the third man said. "I'm sure you remember me, don't you?" I sat silently. I wouldn't say a word to these people. He spoke again. "Ah, maybe not me, but my son possibly? Prince Kaz of Esmery. Ring a bell?" That was when realisation hit me. They were the Royal Family of Esmery. Also known as our rivals. Our enemies. I only recognised Kaz because of school. And his father, King Iras. We learnt about the royal families of Seclari and they were obviously amongst them, as was I. The question still pounded my head, *why am I here?*

"You must be wondering why you are here," Iras said, as if reading my mind. My mouth still stayed shut, not a word being spoken. "You know what gives a king more power over their enemy's country?" he asked. What was he implying? What did he- "Marriage." It all made sense now. They kidnapped me so they could not only have control over me, but control over my kingdom. *Well, they won't be able to force me, will they?*
"I'm never marrying someone that is from your disgusting kingdom," I said, forcing myself to stand up.
"I had a feeling you'd say that," Iras said. Then my eyes followed where Iras was looking. At the staircase. Two guards dragged a girl across the floor, towards me. A girl I knew.
"*Avery!*" I screamed. Her arms were shaking and so were her legs. She had a fresh cut down her face. "*Avery!*" I screamed again. I looked back at Iras and Kaz.
"Father. This wasn't part of the plan," Kaz said, showing concern for my sister.
"Go on deck, *now!*" he said angrily. Kaz left quickly. I knew what I had to do.
"I'll do it," I said. "I'll marry him, but if you touch my sister, then I will not marry him. Do we have a deal?"
"Deal." We shook hands through the bars.
"Now let my sister go," I said firmly. I doubted they'd let her go, but I couldn't risk Avery being in more danger than she was already. I looked at my sister crumpled on the floor, so vulnerable, so weak. Then, Iras left, leaving me with Avery and three guards. The guards unlocked the dungeon gate in front of me. Was the wedding already? I didn't want to get married this quickly. Then the guards threw Avery into the same cell as me. Thank God she was with me.

I didn't trust them. I couldn't forgive myself if she got any more hurt. I held Avery in my arms as she sobbed. Then I realised, *the guards haven't shut the gate*. They were still there though. Just as I was questioning why they left the gate open, two guards came in with three women. And a rack of wedding dresses. I was right. I'm getting married now. The guards left, but the women immediately started dressing me in a magnificent white, floral dress, which fitted me perfectly.

Kaz came to collect me once I was ready. To escort me to my wedding, to somebody who I don't love.

Kaya Odedra (12)

Mr Star

Stars are raised by children on Earth and are sent back to the sky when the time is right.
Now all the stars in the sky are getting ready to launch the baby stars to Earth so they can come back as adults and shine in the sky. "Ten, nine, eight, seven, six, five, four, three, two, one... Launch!" The new generation of stars are travelling to Earth through galaxies, past planets and finally, they get to Earth. Flying through farms, flying overseas, flying through towns and eventually they reach their child guardian.
This story is about a star and its special owner Olivia Woods. All the children over the world have been waiting for their stars to arrive in their bedrooms so they can look after them. After Olivia has been waiting for at least a day, her star finally arrives. Olivia shrieks in excitement as her star flies up to
her. The star is wearing a black top hat and an oversized suit.
"Hello, my name is Olivia, what's your name?" Olivia asks.
"Hi, I'm Leo. Nice to meet you, Olivia," Leo says.
"I'm your star. Your job is to look after me and help me grow. After a year you'll send me back up to the sky and I will shine down upon the Earth," Leo explains.
"I will look after you and keep you safe," Olivia says. "I made this bed for you so you can sleep by me." Tomorrow, Olivia and Leo get to go to school together.
The next morning they eat their breakfast, brush their teeth and get ready for school. At school, Olivia introduces Leo to her friends. "Leo, meet my friends. This is Leila, Isobel, Ava and Scarlett," Olivia introduces.

After their first class, Olivia and Leo are walking down the corridor to put their stuff back in their locker but they run into Jason the bully and his gang. "Look, there's little Olivia and her star, trying to be all fancy and posh with that ugly little hat and oh look at that suit, it doesn't even fit him right," Jason
mocks.
"*Hahahahaha!*" Jason's gang laughs.
"Leave them, alone!" Leila says.
"Yeah, stop being rude!" Scarlett says.
"Go away!" Isobel says.
As Olivia and her friends walk away, Ava asks Olivia if she is okay. Olivia says she is fine, but Leo looks a bit upset. When playtime comes, Olivia tells Leo all about Jason and his gang and how mean they have always been to her.
The next class is about being polite and kind. Jason and Billy (his star) don't care about that lesson and all they're doing is messing around so they don't learn anything.
After school finishes, Leo and Olivia go back home and finish their homework so they can go and play on the park down the road. At the park, Leo and Olivia are playing on the swings when Olivia spots Jason's dad's posh Rolls-Royce pull into the car park. "Oh no, Jason is here. Come on Leo, let's go! We can play in my treehouse instead," Olivia says.
Olivia and Leo spend eleven months together, bonding and comforting each other as Jason and Billy continue to be mean to them.
In just one day's time, Leo and all the other stars will fly back up to the sky.

So they decide to go and play in the treehouse, where they have spent many fun hours together. As bedtime comes they get down from the treehouse and go back inside to get their pyjamas on and go to bed.

After a good night's sleep, they wake up excited but sad as it is time for Leo to fly back up to the sky. Once they finish their breakfast, they get ready to meet up with the other stars so they can make their way back to the sky.

As Olivia and Leo make their way to the launchpads at the bottom of the field they talk about all the happy times they have had together. Finally, they reach the launchpads and Leo finds his. Olivia is crying because Leo is going to leave, but she is happy as they have come so far.

Once everyone has made it to their launchpads the countdown begins. "Ten, nine, eight, seven, six, five, four, three, two, one... Launch!" There is a bright flash as the stars fly into the sky. Olivia opens her eyes to find Leo and Billy lying on the floor in front of their launchpads.

Olivia is shocked and rushes to Leo so they can try again but it still isn't working. They're both confused and start to cry as they think of all the hard work they have accomplished. As Jason walks towards them, he shouts, "You'll never make it!"

Olivia and Leo walk away, deciding to go and sit in the park. As they're walking to the park they overhear Billy and Jason arguing. "You haven't raised me right!" Billy cries.

"I didn't want you here in the first place!" shouts Jason.

As Jason walks away, Billy feels really hurt and starts to cry. Olivia and Leo go over to comfort him. "Do you want to come back to my house?"

Olivia asks.

"Yes please," Billy answers.

Back at Olivia's house, Billy asks if he can stay with Olivia for the week. Olivia says yes and helps Billy to become kind and caring, but in the meantime, Jason has become extremely mean.

As Billy and Leo didn't make it to the sky, they have another chance today. Let's hope they will make it.

At the launchpad, they are surprised as they find Jason, so they ask him what he's doing there. "Oh, I came to tell you that Billy will never make it because I have to press the button," Jason mocks.

Olivia turns around and gasps, "I forgot about that."

"It has to be Jason!" Leo exclaims.

"What are we going to do?" Billy asks.

Jade Buckley (11)

The Elizabeth Express Murder

"Kushii, Kushii!"
I immediately snap out of my daydream to see my dad staring at me. "Sorry, what did you say Dad?" I ask.
"Just asking you what platform our train is?" he replies. I look down at the tickets he handed me and start searching. "We're on platform nine," I say. He asks if I can try and find the platform. It doesn't take me long to spot it and when we arrive, I just stare at the massive train in front of us, it's a snowy white fading to grey but it has a royal purple stripe across the side of it with big white letters saying *The Elizabeth Express.* We hand our tickets to the inspector and then make our way onto the train as I wonder: *what will this trip bring?*
It doesn't take us long to find our cabin and as we open it, I stare and gawp for the second time in less than five minutes. It is the best overnight train compartment I have ever seen... and the only one I have ever seen but that doesn't really matter.
I quickly climb up to the bunk and then start to make myself at home. I reach for my iPad when Dad asks if I want to call Mum, something's wrong with her visa so she can't travel with us. So, I say yes and take the phone from Dad. I call Mum, and we have a little chat but when we say goodbye, I realise we've started moving! I pass the phone back to Dad and he says it's sleeping time, it's only... 9:45... but still! I do what he says anyway though, and it doesn't take long for me to drift off, fast, fast asleep.

When I wake up, I am very hungry. As I get out of bed, I make my way down the ladder to see if Dad's awake. No surprise that he isn't. I check the time on my watch, it's 8:30, the breakfast buffet should be open. I decide to write a little note for my dad before making my way to the breakfast buffet.

When I arrive, there is no one there except for a grumpy man and a girl who looks the same age as me. I decide to grab two small pastries, then I walk over to the girl. "Hi, do you mind if I sit here?" I ask. She looks startled to see me but nods anyway. I start to dig in and finish in less than a minute. I then ask the girl, "What's your name?"

"Gabriela," she says.

"I'm Kushii," I say. Soon we start chatting so much we don't even realise the grumpy man's left. But then we hear a scream, a loud scream.

Me and Gabriela look at each other before rushing to where the sound came from, and we stand there gawping, not believing our eyes. That grumpy man has been... well... murdered! I turn to Gabriela. "We should get help," I speak. She nods and goes off to her cabin.

By the time we get help, I just want to go into my bed. I tell Dad and ask if Gabriela can come too. He says yes, and we walk in shutting the door behind us. "What just happened?" I say, unsure of what to do.

"I think Mr William George III was just murdered," she replies.

I start laughing. "That's his name? William George III?!" I say, unable to stop myself giggling. Soon Gabriela catches on and starts laughing as well.

After a while, we stop and decide that we're going to work out who committed the crime. "Well, when could it have happened?" I ask. We sit there quietly when I remember, "When the lights went off." Gabriela stares at me before remembering as well.

When we go back out again, we hear multiple voices. "Is that William George III?" a posh-sounding lady asks.

"I think so," another lady replies.

I get bored of listening until I hear an upset man cry, "My dear brother!" He soon starts crying on about the universe and gods, when I notice the posh lady has disappeared. I nudge Gabriela and she points to the breakfast buffet. We peek in and see her inside.

An idea then pops into my head. "We should search her cabin while she's out," I whisper.

"But isn't that violating her privacy?" Gabriela asks.

"But what if she's the murderer?" I say. She reluctantly agrees and follows me inside. No one notices we've disappeared.

We start searching when I spot a suitcase with the initials: JR. I tell Gabriela and point. She then looks like a lightbulb might have as well popped over her head. "Jane Rosemary!" she says.

"Who?" I ask. Just as the door behind us swings open.

"What are you doing in here?" Jane Rosemary asks us from behind. We both wince as we turn around, trying to think of an excuse when one pops into my head.

"We were looking for you, Ms Rosemary," I reply, more confident than I feel. She raises an eyebrow at us and scolds us before letting us walk away but I'm sure she was looking worried when we left and I'm going to find out why.

"Who should we check next?" Gabriela asks. I suggest the brother, so we search his cabin. But again, no luck, but this time we don't get caught.

We search the last one but nothing when I remember something. "Maybe the murderer hid the weapon?" Our eyes light up at the same time. We rush to the buffet and start looking when I spot a small bottle with a skull on it, poison! I wave Gabriela over and we piece it all together, Jane Rosemary did it! And she hid the bottle as well! Now we must prove it.

Our little meeting with all the passengers goes great and Jane Rosemary doesn't deny it. Maybe I can do this again next summer break!

Nia Roberts (10)

A Half-Blood's Guide To Quests

Pre-Rules:
The first day is the hardest. That's what everyone told me. But week after week, it just got harder and harder. Now, I'm in this mess. It isn't a pleasant one. I don't want to be in this mess, but you're born into it. It's not a choice. If you were to be in my shoes, you'd probably be dead by now. Like people such as Percy Jackson, I'm a half-blood. Although he has it lucky. He has somewhere where monsters can't get to him. I don't. If you think you might be one, I wouldn't be reading this book. Go home, run, and check underneath your bed. Is it dark? If it is, run. If you're lucky, you can make it to camp. If not... well, we'll get to that later.

People ask me what my name is. It's stupid, it really is. Why do they actually care? It's not like it involves them. But (apparently) I'm rude if I don't tell them. In case you're wondering, it's Luna May Sontonteiro Rodriguez Catan Castadella de le Sonz Bon III. Although it's best to call me Luna.

I would recommend you know how to use a sword if you are one of us. It wouldn't be very easy if you can't fight monsters - almost certain death.

We may have nowhere safe like Percy, but we do have a school. Half-Blood School for Demigods. It's in the UK, for when you don't live near any safety. If you know the right people, then maybe you can be safe. If you're maybe a child of Demeter or Aphrodite then you're not too big a threat, and you won't have to worry. But if you are a child of someone like Ares or the Big Three, Athena, or someone like

them then monsters will come after you when you are about eleven or twelve.
That's enough of an introduction, I should probably get started on the rules to stay alive.

First Rule: Don't Die.
Example: I was walking with my friends, and a cyclops came up to us. He threatened us, so we ran. There wasn't a safe haven for us, so we had to find somewhere it couldn't fit. We ended up in a shady alleyway, where the cyclops couldn't fit. Although, one of us wasn't quick enough, and the cyclops grabbed them. We raised our swords and he threatened to kill Thalia, our friend, and us. We cut him, and he killed Thalia before we could do anything. Cynthia, behind me, couldn't do anything, and neither could Sam. It was only me standing up to this bully.
"Go away and pick on someone your own weight!"
"Then there won't be anyone to pick on!" he complained.
"*That's the point!*"

Second Rule: Don't Anger Gods.
We all ran away from the cyclops, but Cynthia bumped into Ares, and Ares didn't wake up on the right side of the bed.
"Watch it before I turn you into a tapeworm!" he snapped. His voice was gravelly, like Batman.
"How about you pick on someone your own weight!" she snapped back at him.
"Cynthia! We say that to enemies who killed our friends, not gods!" I was nervous now. Sure enough, he turned her into a tapeworm and ran her over with his Harley.

"Scram!" He drove forward on his Harley, so me and Sam jumped out of the way.

Third Rule: Don't Go To The Lotus Casino - Ever!
We ran to the nearest building and said that we were lost. The man said we could stay at the casino and there was a phone in there. We went inside, and it looked so cool! There was a ten-storey water slide, a gift shop, games, VRs, free food, everything you can imagine was there. They gave us green casino cards and showed us to our room. It was massive, with a fifty-inch TV, two massive king beds, an ensuite, everything you could ask for, even a hot tub!
"Maybe we could... uh... stay a while?" I said.
"Maybe..." We stayed there for a few days, enjoying games and food, everything in the gift shop... By those few days we were decked out in Lotus Casino merch, even stuff we didn't need: pencil cases, stationery, notebooks, cuddly toys, keyrings, backpacks... pretty much the whole store.
We came out maybe a month later, and we picked up a newspaper on the way out. Although, when we came out, it wasn't 2024. It was 2059. It was only a while later we realised it was because there was a time stop there, that's how it felt like a few months when it was... years.

Rule Four: Don't Summon Hellhounds.
Somehow, when we walked out, a hellhound was right in front of us, ready to attack. Sam brought out her bow, and I brought out my sword. I did close range attacks whilst she covered long range attacks. I cut its leg but it bit my arm. It was all bloody and sore. I screamed, but no one cared. Sam finished off the hellhound with an arrow to the heart. We walked to a taxi, and we went back to the school.

All of the kids were really excited, then realised that two of us had died. They seemed disappointed, and the teachers burned their shrouds. Sam and I are famous now, but not in a good way.

Important! Rule Five: Don't Go On Quests And Come Back When People Are Dead.
Everyone looked at us funny, like we were noobs, but I don't think they realised how important this quest was. We got an apple from the Hesperides, which is no easy quest when you have two newbies with you. Me and Sam had been there a while, but honestly, that was probably the hardest quest I've been on, mainly because I had to fight a dragon on my own, because no one else would help. I probably should've written that down too - I'll do that next time.

Grace Green (11)

2020

I turned in my bed, still far away from the world. The only thing that drove me back to reality was the creaking of the bedframe and an unfamiliar, ululating beeping sound. I sighed in exasperation, heaving myself upwards and throwing the duvet off of my body.

I had thought the beeping sound might have come from the car factory a few doors down from us. Then I remembered about the outside world. The morning sun was already high in the sky, having risen ages ago. The birds had finished their morning song and I couldn't hear Mother or Father below me. Sunday school would soon be starting.

I turned to look at my travelling clock perched on my worn, wooden bedside table. However, I was met with a small, rectangular device, no bigger than a small box of chocolates. It flashed at me in large, red numbers; separated by a meek colon inbetween. The time wasn't what scared me or caught my attention. In small letters, right in the corner of the screen, was the date. I had known that day as the 24th of June 1920. But the clock clearly read '24th of June 2020'. 2020? That couldn't be right. That was a century away. And yet, a horrible, queasy feeling grew in my stomach that something hadn't felt right from the moment I had opened my eyes that morning.

I hadn't a clue what to do. My mind fluttered with possibilities. Though it was warm, a shiver ran down my spine. I shuddered.

The bleeping had stopped. The flashing numbers on the clock had stopped. Though the date disappeared, I didn't forget about it. The bleeping had been coming from the clock. Unsettling, foreboding silence filled the room.

I called to Mother and Father. No reply. I couldn't hear them down the stairs, or anywhere in the house. It was strange - Mother was almost always home, looking after me and my brother. She hadn't... forgotten about me? She was probably dropping off my brother to Sunday School at this very moment. If I left now, I could probably get there just in time. They would have to excuse my bedraggled appearance. I made the decision to not think about the clock or date anymore. However, though I tried my utmost hardest, I couldn't quite shake the thought.

I had finally half-distracted myself from it until I went to open my door. As I tried to swing it open, something was stopping it from opening. Someone. I could only just about see who through the inch the door had opened by. Two men stood outside my door, stopping me from getting outside, dressed all in black. Were they liveried footmen? No... We couldn't afford that. Something wasn't adding up. They both had a cloth of fabric across their nose and mouth - then secured by a fine string looping around their ears. Why?

"I need to go! I'm late!"

They did not move. They did not hear. Their eyes were open, but it was like they could not see. I was trapped in my room, with no escape. A feeling of fright crept up on me. The silence of the room was deafening. The room seemed to grow smaller. I felt suffocated. Questions poured into my mind, flowing freely like a waterfall. I drowned in the river below.

I had no other option. I reached up to the window and threw it open carelessly. I was met with an oppressive gale that swept into the room, whipping my hair into my face. It was strange. It was a beautiful day - the sun was shining, the weather was warm and the birds were singing. But nobody was outside. They were all in their houses; as if they were put into isolation.

I pulled myself up onto the window ledge and perched myself on it. The air engulfed my nostrils. I gulped down the cool air. It tasted delicious. It tasted delicious until it didn't. It was grim, acerbic. It made my face contorted with disgust. I coughed, my lungs also contorting at the taste. It reached the back of my throat, travelling through my body. I was infected.

I slipped off of the windowsill and back onto the floor of my bedroom before my legs buckled beneath me. I saw myself sitting in a heap in the mirror opposite to me. My face was deathly pale. My hair was frightfully messy in the harsh wind that still circled my room. The air wouldn't leave me alone. It continued to fly around my room, draining life out of me by the second.

With all the strength I could muster, I clawed my way to the door and screamed as loud as I could. "Help." It came out as quiet as a breath of the wind.

My body screamed in protest for me to stop. I gave in. With the small amount of life left inside of me, I carved 'I love you' on the wall with my fingernail. Hopefully, my family would find it. They would know I had loved them. But I had travelled a century forward in time. Was I even in the same time period as my parents?

There was nothing I could do. The room around me became blurred and my eyes fluttered shut. I felt weak. The wind took my final drop of life. I lay still - unblinking, unmoving. I couldn't feel anything. Everything went black...

She had been transported a century forward in time. To 2020, to the time of the pandemic and the disease Coronavirus. Her parents never found her message and their memories were wiped about her ever living. She had experienced the world in which people in 2020 had lived in - people isolated in their homes, not being able to even leave their room if they had it or were at risk of infecting somebody else. Mask-wearing and the infamous, airborne disease. She died of Coronavirus when she opened the window.

Sophia Jacobs (11)

Deserted

Why did it have to be me and May who were stranded on a deserted island in the middle of the ocean? We were always getting ourselves into tight situations, however this was different. I could still see where we had laid the remains of the once successful rowing boat on the sand. As usual, this was all May's fault.
"Why did you have to get into a temper like you always do, and drag us out here in that pathetic rowing boat?!" I exploded, breaking the silence.
"Excuse me! I'm not the one with the temper," May retorted accusingly.
"That's it!" I exclaimed, and before I knew it I was running as fast as my legs could carry me - away from May.
I had all the time in the world to ponder what had happened, so I did. Reluctantly, I turned back the way I had come and bumped straight into May. She hurtled to the ground, covering her dark brown hair with fallen leaves. Heaving herself up, she panted, "We're going home, come quick!"
My body felt like it would overflow with joy as I scrambled after May, who had an uncanny knack for getting out of trouble. That was until I saw what she meant by were going home. Two sleek, grey dolphins were waiting patiently next to the very same rocks on which our boat had been dashed to pieces. May knew very well how terrified I was of creatures of all kinds. I was already getting fidgety.
"Two words: no and no," I stated bluntly, though my hands trembled.

May was already in the sea, climbing onto the larger dolphin. I noted the blue tint to her lips. "Please, April, do it for me," she begged, and I knew I couldn't possibly refuse. I took a deep breath, then reached one exhausted leg over the back of the dolphin, put my arms around it and hung on. I couldn't quite believe that May had managed to force me into the sea yet again.

As the dolphins bobbed up and down through the salty waves, I clung on with all my might, resisting the urge to scream. Beside me, May whooped and cheered, as if she was on a fairground ride. My drenched blonde hair was plastered to my neck and I shivered violently, unable to take it anymore. I shakily opened my mouth, loosening my grip on the dolphin and stopped dead. I squinted through the fog, checking that I hadn't been mistaken. *No.* My spirits rose almost to the heavens. In the distance, the silhouette of an enormous boat was wreathed in mist. Our last hope.

I began to yell, "Here! We're here! Help us, please! We're here!" I waved my arms frantically, my energy renewed. May dug her nails into my arm and dragged it down. I frowned at her, bewildered.

"We can't go on that boat. I have a bad feeling about it. I recognise that very boat, and not in a good way," she protested.

I had to make a decision, and quickly, else there would be no chance of ever seeing home again. "I'm sorry, May," I whispered softly, and carried on towards the approaching boat.

As I got closer, the less sure I got. The boat had huge, ragged sails along with a rotting mermaid figurehead bearing pointed teeth. I couldn't turn back now. My body was numb, my fingers were wrinkled, and my knuckles were white from gripping so hard. That was when I noticed a tall

man on the deck of the boat. He was easily six feet tall, with two impossibly sly eyes set close together.
"You down there! You look half drowned! Come up here, my crew'll get you some hot cocoa," the man offered, in what he clearly thought was an inviting voice. He swiftly hung a rope ladder down the side of the boat and stood, waiting.
It was my only option. In my hurry to get off of the dolphin, I forgot to think about what the mysterious man could actually have been planning.
I struggled up the rope ladder and fell in a sopping heap on the deck. The man hoisted the ladder up after me, cutting off all possibilities of escape.
"I recognise you. You are the daughter of pure evil. Your father did unspeakable things to me, and I swore to get my revenge. Fate has played you like a chess piece into my hands. Though I have no idea how you got out here, you will never return," he grinned maliciously. He bound my wrists and ankles with harsh twists of rope and shoved me into a musty cabin; locking the door.
I ought to have listened to May, I knew by now that she was a born leader, and could save anyone's life if she put her mind to it, though why she would ever want to save mine after the day's happenings was a mystery to me. Maybe I should've expected bad luck. After all, today I had now been thirteen for thirteen days.
Just as I gave in to the fact that the cruel man's words had been true, the door creaked open. My heart beat double time. I saw a pale hand clutching a hairpin peek around the edge of the door, followed by a familiar cheeky grin.

"May!" I breathed, delighted. I had never been so happy to see her before. She held a finger to her lips and slipped out of the door.
I followed her, and within seconds we were out on deck. May let down the rope ladder, nimbly climbed down it and retook her seat on the dolphin. I did the same, this time not minding in the least. "Why did you come back for me?" I asked breathlessly.
"Despite all our arguments, you're my sister," May replied sincerely.
Nothing mattered anymore, not even the vast ocean we had to brave, because we were together.

Eva Bryant (10)

Otters' Uprising

Part One

It was a dark, stormy night. The Earth's spirits dozed. The surface was once bustling but now it was another story. Under the sea where a new world was uncovered lived a group of tyrants named the sharks who ruled over the weaker group of creatures called the otters with an iron fist. That very day an important event occurred. The leader of the merciless sharks, whom himself had claimed the throne, was sitting down holding the very sword that many of the otters were slaughtered with. This is the story of the otters' uprising.

"Where is my attendant who I sent to imprison that protesting otter?" moaned Lord Shark.

"Here he is, Your Majesty," yelled Lord Shark.

"Sorry, I'm just trying to tell you that I caught the otter and you shall feast on him but the otter's brother escaped, Your Majesty," said Lord Shark's attendant.

"Good," replied Lord Shark.

"Sorry to interrupt you but King Otter wants to talk to you," interrupted his second bodyguard.

"Not that weak old bounty hunter," moaned Lord Shark.

"Hello, this is King Otter speaking," spoke King Otter confidently.

"What do you want from me?" questioned Lord Shark.

"Nothing but freedom."

"*Never!*" boomed Lord Shark.

"Look, I know you hate us, but you've got to stop this. Remember when we were friends and worked together? We accomplished a lot till the orcas separated us and you regained us like a tyrant. You need to destroy this now before it destroys you, old friend," spoke King Otter wisely.

"You were always a smooth talker, King Otter, but it's not going to work on me. You were once my partner and now are a bounty hunter in an alleyway, what a downfall," spoke Lord Shark villainously but not wisely.

Moments later, King Otter slammed the phone down. "So, he has taken the hard way out," he whispered. "I'll make him pay," he added. "Summon the royal scaredy cat bodyguards!" he shouted.

"Sorry but they aren't royal, remember we are inferior and are reigned over," reminded his smartest chairman.

"*Just summon them please!*" he shouted for the first time. "This is it, this is the uprising of otters," he shouted in triumph although they were still not free.

Part Two

The scaredy cat bodyguards marched out of the alleyway, all with a bounty on Lord Shark himself. They were going to take revenge but there was a shark spy deployed in the alleyway who figured out that the otters were about to take revenge. "Lord Shark, Lord Shark, Your Majesty, the otters plan revenge on you!" the spy shouted.

"Thank you James Bond the Shark 007," replied Lord Shark. "So, it's a clash they want, now you're talking. I declare Ocean World War I!" he shouted.

Chaos began outside as soldiers began to start their formations and the rebel state emblem was raised by the scaredy cat bodyguards who were now soldiers. "*With the splash of a wave, I declare Ocean World War I!*" Lord Shark yelled. Coral bombs and grand mines with Sea-4 were dropped. This truly was the darkest of times. The Pacific hotels and undersea beaches were blown up. Otter terrorists blew up the statue of the shark. The ocean was engulfed in a wildfire of death.

Then amidst the destruction the orca council found out this was the time when they could strike, and it would be easier to notice a beetle in a lump of spiders than this. So, they decided to let Experiment 666, the Kraken out. The sharks and otters were at war when the large Kraken began laying waste to the capital city called Slaughter Mania Devils State. "Lord Shark, I warned you. Your villainous war has hammered us into certain doom!" he shouted. "We have to work together."

"Never since the age of the dinosaurs will I work with you!" Lord Shark yelled.

"It's our last chance," King Otter warned.

"Fine," Lord Shark agreed. "King Otter, distract the Kraken, I'll send the forces to disarm it and I am going to climb up to the most dangerous part, the eye."

"Yes, old friend," he replied.

Lord Shark climbed to the eye with all his might and did the one thing he never did. He asked politely. "Kraken, please, stop, we can be friends. Perhaps I can take you to the megalodon coffee shop and we can have a cup of coffee each?" he asked.

The Kraken, having heard this, stopped in its tracks. It lowered its hostages and shrank till it was a humble octopus.

"You did it, Lord Shark, you showed kindness for once in your life!" King Otter yelled in triumph.

"Yes, it feels all nice. You know what, I declare me and King Otter both leaders which means you have gained your freedom!" he announced in triumph.
To this day, the octopus means peace under the sea.

Muhammad Arfeen Fazal (10)

A Solution To Climate Change?

My shivering feet pulled me towards the frosty city. Lodgings, which were once full of protection and warmth, now abandoned just like the rest of the desolate space. Imagine: a hypothermic, companionless, deserted world. This was what I was suffering. Outside, I was quivering with the never-ending fear of staying here. (Inside, I felt many more emotions: downhearted, anxious, horrified). I started searching for a door that would lead me to food, warmth, and shelter. If the snow had not been as impactful, if they had not abandoned their houses, if they had forgotten to lock their doors, then my wishes would have come true. However, I knew that if my wishes did not come true, I would be taken by the disastrous environment and would have a significantly high chance of death. *Come on*, I thought. *Just one door! Please! Come on, come on...* With that, the world around me disappeared.

A delightful smell of roses brought me back to my senses. Many questions fluttered to my overwhelmed head. *Where am I? Did I escape the icy city? Am I safe now?* Slowly but steadily, I opened my fragile eyes. Almost immediately, I realised where I was. Hospital. I was crowded with two people standing around me, one of whom I guessed to be a doctor. However, the second person was not someone whom I remembered. Flummoxed, exhausted, petrified, I realised someone must have rescued me - but who?

"Hello, Isaac. How are you? You fainted when someone found you," the doctor, who seemed more anxious about me than I was, asked compassionately.

I responded, "I'm good, thanks. What happened to the frozen city?"

"Now, now, we can answer these questions at a different time," the other figure, who reminded me of Dad, calmed my nerves. "Now you get some rest." With that, each member departed, leaving me to gather my thoughts whilst motionless as if paralysed by whatever traumatic event placed me here in this state.

"I'm in hospital," I interpreted. "I notice there's a person who's a bit like Dad. I've been rescued from the frozen city, probably from him too. Well, the tiredness is creeping over me, so goodnight." And with that, I fell into a deep slumber, vowing to uncover the mystery of how I emerged from there unscathed.

Days passed as I was stuck in the lively yet crowded hospital. I was recovering rapidly, and, in a few days, I would be released.

"In around a week on the 3rd of May," the innocent doctor informed me.

"On the 3rd of May?" I whispered to myself. "Wasn't it September?" I noticed a calendar on a nearby wall. Squinting, I was shocked at the date. "1985?! Wait," I pondered over the thought, "is Dad really Dad, just younger?" I was rudely interrupted by another doctor. This one hadn't checked up on me before - what were his intentions?

"Hello Isaac, I have some good news for you," the doctor announced. "You may leave."

I was overjoyed - I started to beam with the realisation that I could leave the boundaries which confined me to this spot - I was free. The more I thought about it, the more delighted I became.

Surprisingly, instead of showing this, I muttered with a hint of desperation, "I will never again meet the friends I made in here." Nevertheless, once I was prepared, I stepped out into the modern age.

I stepped out into a bustling city. Many sights reminded me of how life once was: as busy and great as it was. The skyscraping buildings towered over me as my shock of being in the past melted into pure excitement. The glistening sun beamed over me as passers-by continued along their daily lives. I decided to start searching for a map that would guide me somewhere tranquil. I located a map and desired to visit a luscious forest.

Once I arrived, I instantly realised my suspicions were correct. The forest was mesmerising and majestic. The intoxicating smell of the appetising berries enchanted me to go deeper into the forest. The inside of the forest was as astounding as the outside. If the snow hadn't been as impactful, if people had cared about the environment, if we hadn't used plastic so much, then my world might have been like this. I realised that if I promoted to stop using plastic, I could have a world like that. But could I achieve my goal? Would my voice even be heard?

I wondered whether I was destined for this. Questions buzzed into my head; some were swiftly followed by answers. *How will I do this? By protesting in parliament or starting a charity? Will I be stuck in this time now? Probably. Can I really do this?* The answer didn't come. I remained with the minuscule (yet existent) hope in my plan.

The more I attempted to make a change, the more of a chance I could create for my dream world to become true. One more question came to my restless mind.
Will the world listen to what I have to say?

Senuka Fernando (10)

My Camp At The Cam

Skipping ecstatically, I thought about the wonderful days I just had. It was Wednesday, my favourite Wednesday of the year as we were going on a camping trip. As we got into the coach, Miss Peach, who is my very wise form tutor despite the name, made an announcement. "On the trip, you will have partners who you always have to be with when you go out of your tent." A million names flew through my head. Could I be with Sam Riddles or Jack Humphrey or Charlie Mynar?! "Before we get there," Miss Peach continued, "I will give you one clue, there is a boys' tent and a girls' tent so if you're a girl you'll be with a girl and vice-versa!" Everyone cheered as my shoulders slumped, eyes drooped and sighed. You see, I feel more comfortable around boys than girls. After what felt like an eternity, we arrived at our camp at the river Cam. The trees waved at us and the Cam gave us a glimpse of her sparkling surface. We did lots of activities in the radiating, ruby-like river including: kayaking and paddleboarding; swimming and saving; and pedaloes and fishing (but carefully unhooking and freeing the fish afterwards, but I swear I saw Arabella sneak a few into her pocket).

Somewhere in the middle of the amazing, astounding and astonishing activities we had lunch and afterwards we had dinner. After that though, we did another activity (well two, to be fair). First, Miss Peach told us our partners. I was with Anjali and she is quite nice to be honest. She's a bit like me but doesn't have many friends, girls and boys, so definitely not gregarious, and so she was jumping with joy when I got out my friendship bracelet kit and made my first ever bracelet, a best friend one for Anjali! We also got to roast marshmallows, which were as sweet as strawberries, and make smores!

Then, after the smores and the songs around the campfire, we got into our tents to sleep. Arabella, my arch-enemy, decided to read so we had to leave the lights on. She went on whimpering like a scared kitten about a Cam monster in the river but I couldn't imagine such a horrendous thing emerging from the capturing Cam river.

After a while, when still no one had slept because of the lights, there was a *Boom! Thud!* "*Argh!*"

"Argh, it's the Cam monster!" screamed Sophie, the coward who would believe anything.

"Ha, I told you so losers!" cackled Arabella rudely, blowing a raspberry.

I didn't believe them so I went outside, with Anjali as Miss Peach had told us. Almost as soon as we went out we rushed back in. Arabella had a look on her face that said, *scared, are you?!* We grabbed our torches and the face went away. She whispered something to Sophie and they sniggered and cackled menacingly.

We rushed outside with our torches and found Miss Peach looking furious. She asked us why the lights were on and I answered truthfully that, "Arabella was reading her book and was trying to frighten us by saying there was a Cam monster." I usually hated and regretted being a tell-tale but a teacher (my favourite one) was asking me a question and I had to answer truthfully.

"I definitely heard all the other ways she oppressed you!" exclaimed Miss Peach, turning as red as a tomato and fists clenching. She stormed into the tent telling Arabella she was in detention and couldn't participate in the rest of the activities. "You are also to sleep with me in my tent!" shouted Miss Peach, waking up the boys who had been sleeping peacefully.

Arabella gaped at Miss Peach but still obeyed her by switching off the light as she left. Sophie turned and glared at me. Her nickname was now Spiteful Sophie, not Scared Sophie.

At the break of dawn, when the birds were singing, loud yawns were to be heard. Who were they? Why they were us of course! I woke up remembering my revenge on Arabella and smiled. Best school trip ever!

I ran over to the campfire like everybody else and tried to find the best log. After we all settled down (apart from Arabella as she had been sent home) Miss Peach had an announcement to make, but this time it was a good one! She invited me and Anjali to come to her and we received Miss Peach's special but rare smell stickers that were given to 'only amazing and brave pupils'. She made us tell the rest of the year about what had happened last night and she told us we were very brave to have gone outside expecting a monster. She also told us that we were trustworthy and sensible for going out of the tent together and telling her the truth. Anjali and I stuck our spectacularly smelling stickers on our friendship bracelets to remember that awesome trip.

So here I am, today, walking to school with my best friend, beaming from ear to ear that we were the first-ever pupils to get smell stickers.

Neha Sathiyamoorthy (9)

Mayhem At The Monster

The Fun Time Funfair was overflowing with awestruck ride-enthusiasts, splashing their hard-earned money on chocolatey, chewy churros and other overpriced delicacies. The sun gazed over the park, which was equipped with an abundance of thrilling rides along with a plethora of less intense rides for young adventurers.

The whistling wind harmonised with screams of delight, creating a symphony of joy. The aroma of buttery popcorn thronged in the air, enveloping the air like a comforting blanket. The pungent scent of countless deep-fried foods also slithered in the park, accompanied by energetic music being pumped out by the noisy arcades. Children dragged their parents through the boundless park like obedient pets. Entering the Fun Time Funfair was like crossing the bridge into a different world.

As the moon appeared its weary eyes placed themselves upon the fair, overlooking even the tallest rides. Amongst these select few attractions, one stood out the most - 'The Monster'. This behemoth of a roller coaster had intimidating red eyes, a bewilderingly long drop and a queue that trickled past all the alluring food stands.

Meanwhile, a herd of thrill-seekers boarded the purple cart, which had a green lightning bolt down both sides. The wheels departed, startling the passengers, and further tightening disaster's grip. The clicking of the chains, as the cart ascended, further intensified the suspense.

As they completed the jaw-dropping arch, it stopped. The people inside the cart jittered, snapping their heads around. As it started its descent, screams of people on and next to the ride could be heard. Faces of awe quickly turned into faces of horror at the events unfolding before them. The cart derailed. It flew into the air accompanied by the audible sound of gasps from the bystanders below. It crashed into a stand. Flames engulfed the cart, inciting chaos in the park. Fortunately, other than being traumatised, no life-changing damage was inflicted upon the scarred - in more ways than one - adventurers. A young boy was seen emerging from the rubble as his family ran to help him. Luckily, it only rolled once and just glided on the ground because of the wheels. Most crowds fled the scene like frightened cattle, as flocks of police cars flooded the gates. The wailing of the sirens mingled with the shutters of the camera and the news reporters to create an overwhelming cacophony of stress. However, the emergency services weren't alone. Gliding through the crowds, which were like clouds in a concrete sky, a slim, ominous man strode forward, unfazed by the spectacular episode that had just taken place. He marched through the groups of people, accompanied by dramatic gasps. He was a profiler for the FBI. The menacing figure, who had wispy hair and a chiselled jaw, proceeded through the cool breeze sporting a remarkably long trench coat. It seemed old yet new, vintage yet modern and was accompanied by a crimson fedora. His controlled breathing echoed in the air which was still littered with the distant smell of cotton candy.

After crossing a few reporters and entering the central hub, he went into a cosy office with a large bookshelf with books ranging from Shakespeare to Jules Verne. Against the window overlooking the crash, a mahogany table with countless decorations. In the room, there were four people. His entrance startled them awake and they were taken by surprise by his appearance. He placed his gentle gaze on everyone.

He approached the man closest to him as he grunted in disapproval. "Before you ask anything, it wasn't me! I know that I'm the head engineer but what could I possibly gain from this? What a load o- load of... nonsense," he exclaimed. The profile stared daggers at him, squinting his eyes at him. The head engineer, Richmond, proceeded. "And I wasn't there in the first place, I was buying guitar picks for my gig, which I'm late for now! I came as soon as I heard the news," Richmond uttered, passing him a box of picks.

He moved on, interviewing the rest of them. All of their arguments made sense, except for one. Upon request, he was brought files of everyone's background and conveniently, Richmond, was sent wire transfers of absurd amounts of money from an encrypted account which led to Fun Time's biggest competitor: The Funtasticals.

"Richmond, you're under arrest!" the profiler exclaimed.

"I was buying picks!"

"If you bought them today, why is this one faded and scratched?" he queried. "And as it turns out, you really needed to repay that loan, isn't that right?"

As Richmond was preparing to speak, the profiler revealed a dozen more scratched picks. The police ran towards him, but he didn't resist. They cuffed him, dragging him through the maze of tables and off into the sunset.

Sacha Imankerdjo Lambert (11)

Visiting My Grandparents

Taking a trip to the Netherlands by train to visit your grandparents is a once-in-a-lifetime experience. Just imagine yourself on the train, perhaps at the break of dawn as the sun rises, casting a golden, glimmering glow over the Dutch landscape. As the train quietly approaches the station, you witness the lush, green environment, quaint villages and peaceful, tranquil canoes.

You might see crops growing in large quantities swaying to the wind or a flock of birds soaring high in the air as their wing tips part the sky. Inside the train, there's a comfortable sensation that tugs onto you when nearing your destination. The anticipation builds in you as you can see your grandparents' town near the horizon. The scenery may shift between bicycles in rows waiting for an individual to use them or the locals carrying on their normal day-to-day life. Stepping off the train, your nose would be overwhelmed by the fresh aroma of bread and Dutch treats from the nearby bakeries.

Approaching your grandparents' house, there is a feeling of warmth and joy in your stomach which tells you something... You are going to enjoy yourself.

Mohamed Mahamed (11)

The True Story Of The Three Little Pigs: As Told By The Wolf

Let me introduce myself. My name is John (a bit like Elton John), also known as The Big Bad Wolf but this isn't a true representation of me. Let me tell you what really happened on that fateful day, involving the kerfuffle with the pigs.
I was just sitting down near my fire, relaxing my legs, doing a crossword. I was enjoying the peace and quiet, drinking a cup of nettle tea. Just then, my dog, Powder, started barking, which obviously meant she wanted to go for a walk. I got up, put my neon yellow welly boots on, grabbed my umbrella and Powder's extendable lead from the shoe cupboard, and unlocked my heavy wooden door.
Powder was really excited and hyper to be out in the fresh air and rain (because she loves puddles!) and she pulled me up the road to my neighbour's house. Now I hadn't met this neighbour before because he'd only just moved in, but I had heard some interesting gossip about him (wink, wink!). Apparently, he was chased out of his old house because of the trouble he was causing!
All of a sudden, Powder and I stumbled across this house, which was strangely made of hay! I was dreadfully embarrassed because Powder decided to do his business outside the house, so I walked up the garden path and gently knocked on the door, afraid to break it as it was so fragile.

When I got there, I shouted, "Hello there, I'm terribly sorry to disturb you. I hope I haven't interrupted your dinner. I just wanted to introduce myself and I wondered if you have a spare poo bag because my dog, Powder, has inconveniently done a poo in front of your mailbox."
"Yes, actually you have really interrupted me. I'm trying to cut my toenails in peace!"
I apologised for the inconvenience and turned to walk away, but he slammed the door shut behind me. I heard a rumbling sound and turned to see the straw house falling down into one big pile, and the pig was suffocated under the straw.
I was so scared that I might get the blame that I just ran away, wherever Powder led me. I had such a stitch!
After what seemed like an eternity, we arrived at a little stick house on the edge of a sunny village. I leaned on the post box belonging to this house, in order to catch my breath, when all of a sudden the post box fell down! A window opened in the house and a pig's face appeared at the blinds and said, "Oi you! What do you think you're doing down there?"
"Oh, I'm ever so sorry. It was an accident. Little pig, little pig, please let me in and we can sort things out I'm sure."
"Not by the hairs on my chinny chin chin, I will not let you in!"
I am quite an anxious wolf and when someone shouts at me, I get very nervous and panicky. In order to get my breathing under control, I do some breathing techniques I learned in my yoga class. I breathed in through my nose for five counts, and then blew out my breath for ten counts, but I accidentally blew the whole house down! I couldn't believe that this was the second house I'd seen collapse in the same

day, on the same estate! I thought it would look really suspicious if I were caught looking at dead pigs, so I decided it was best to continue with Powder's walk.

We walked alongside a bluebell hollow trying to get home a quick way, but then I stumbled upon a large, brown brick house which was nestled in some trees. It had a sign outside of it saying *Therapy Studio*. As soon as I saw the sign, a big wave of guilt washed over me. I decided to be a brave boy and go in there and confess my accidents. I rang the *Ring* doorbell, and I froze on the spot when the door was opened. There in front of me was another pig who looked exactly like the ones I had just (*accidentally*) killed! I told him everything on the doorstep before I went into the house and asked him if I could come in.

"No, you're not allowed in here. I'm afraid you might kill me!" shouted the therapist, slamming the door.

I really wanted to explain what happened, but he wouldn't let me in, no matter how many times I asked. I saw a ladder leaning up against the side of the house, so I decided to climb up it and go in through the chimney. But the mean pig had lit a fire and put on a big pot of water to boil. Unfortunately for me, I didn't see it in time. The first I knew of it was when I landed with a big splash! My bum was burning! I leapt up, grabbing my bum cheeks, and ran out of the door as fast as lightning!

As I was running down the road, the police pulled up and arrested me and accused me of murdering two pigs. Can you believe it?

That is how I got to be known as the Big Bad Wolf.

Darcy Bickford-Kehoe (10)

Ancient Greece

I will tell you now a little story
And I hope this will bring me glory.
I will explain to you how
The ancient Greeks lived and survived.
They had simple houses,
Of course with little tiny mice.
There were courtyards with all the rooms around
With no women allowed.
The marketplace was crowded
And many people came to sell and buy things, talking aloud.
Olympic games were held every four years
Where athletes kept fit with no tears.
The highest mountain was called Olympus,
This was home to gods, religion and symbols.
All the ports were really busy,
People with boats catching fish but getting dizzy.
You can see amazing objects in the museum,
Vases, bowls and silver coins - premium!
Ancient Greek architecture
Was the best with the temples' texture.
Athens was the richest city,
On the top of the hill, a huge temple - looking pretty.
That temple was called the Acropolis
And made Athens Greece's metropolis.

Alexander Ivanov (9)

The Creature

It was a stormy night, the kind that sent shivers down spines and made hearts race with fear. The wind howled angrily outside, battering against the windows and creating an unsettling atmosphere. We were all scared stiff, tightly cocooned beneath our thick duvets, seeking comfort and warmth against the onslaught of the storm.
Suddenly, a gigantic creak reverberated through the house, echoing ominously as if something was shifting in the very structure itself. Then came another creak, and yet another, each sound rippling through the air like whispered warnings of impending doom.
In an instant, a bright light cut through the darkness, penetrating our makeshift sanctuary of duvets. Our eyes widened in shock; it was as if the very night had been torn apart by this sudden illumination. But just as quickly as the light had appeared, it vanished, plunging us back into darkness.
The stifling silence returned, thick and suffocating, until it was shattered by a deafening *smash*. The sound of glass shattering on the ground resonated through the air, a chaotic symphony of echoes, followed by what seemed like heavy footsteps, pounding rapidly as if something - or someone - was approaching. Panic surged through us, and in that moment of pure terror, we made an instinctive decision... *Run!*
We ran and ran, our lungs burning and our muscles screaming in protest, each footfall pounding against the ground in agony. The adrenaline pushed us forward, but the fear that gripped us could be felt in the air, a thick fog that clouded our thoughts.

The dark, cold woods enveloped us, the trees' twisted branches reaching out like skeletal fingers. All we had to protect ourselves were our clothes and scarves, feeble barriers against the chill of the night and the overwhelming uncertainty that loomed around us.
Eventually, exhaustion took hold, and we searched for a sanctuary amongst the chaos. Eventually we found a small clearing, and huddled closely together on the earthy ground, hoping to find some semblance of rest despite the fear clawing at our minds. The wind howled mournfully, a haunting sound that seemed to echo our own fears. We tried in vain to block out the whispering of the trees, our rustling leaves carrying secrets we dared not understand. Erica, overcome with emotion, was sobbing quietly, tears streaming down her cheeks as she longed desperately for her parents, feeling lost and abandoned in the gloom. Her brother, Mick, sat beside her, leaning in to embrace her tightly, desperately trying to comfort her with gentle words and soothing reassurances. Meanwhile, Alan K and I stood guard protectively, our senses heightened as we scanned the dark treeline for any sign of the *creature* that haunted our thoughts. Nora, exhausted from the night's ordeal, had drifted off to sleep, blissfully dreaming of her warm, cosy bed and her beloved teddy bear, Bodym, oblivious to the terror enveloping the rest of us.
As morning's light began to filter through the trees, it was a striking contrast to the oppressive atmosphere of the night before. Yet, despite the sun's rays attempting to break through the canopy, there were no cheerful bird songs to greet the new day and rouse the five of us from our slumber.

Alan K, the self-appointed leader among us, seemed to feel an overwhelming need to stir everyone awake, seeing it as his duty to rally the group for what lay ahead. We needed to embark on a perilous hike, a journey into the unknown, but the destination was still shrouded in uncertainty. Which way should we go?

After a heated 'discussion', we agreed to head east, believing that it was the furthest direction from the house, hopeful that the unknown roads ahead held the promise of escape.

With a collective resolve, we began our trek once more, walking through the dense underbrush and navigating the twisting pathways that revealed themselves in the daylight. Our stomachs began to rumble and grumble as hunger gnawed at us, yet on we pressed, surviving on the berries and nuts we could scavenge along the way.

Hours passed, and as the sun reached its highest point, illuminating the forest around us, desperation began to creep into our hearts. We were exhausted, worn thin by the trials of the day, and each step felt heavier than the last as we yearned for something more substantial to eat and a place to rest, our bodies pleading for relief from the relentless pace of our journey.

But little did we know that our journey had just begun...

Christopher O'Dornan (11)

The Friendship Story

Once upon a time in a happy family, there lived a dog and cat called Jefry and Cathy. They were the best of friends. But one day they had the biggest fight in the world ever! Then Cathy ran to the back door. Jefry was confused. Jefry raced after Cathy but when Jefry got outside Cathy was not to be found.

Jefry was very sad that his old friend was missing. *What if she never comes back?* Jefry knew that she would never come back and she never did.

Three months passed and Cathy had not come back. Now Jefry was the saddest dog in the world. Jefry didn't know that Cathy lived in a box. He knew Cathy was sad and alone. He also knew that Cathy had no food to eat. Their parents were worried. Cathy grew quite old and still.

But one day Jefry saw Cathy. Cathy said, "Jefry, is that you?" "Yes," said Jefry. Jefry picked up Cathy and brought her inside. Their parents were so pleased and they lived happily in the best house with a happy life.

Wren Jervis-McNamara (6)

The Missing Parents

Once upon a time, lived a boy called Sam. He had short brown hair and bright blue eyes that sparkled. Sam lived in a cosy, little bungalow with his kind and hard-working mum and dad. His dad was a daring explorer, always seeking new adventures, while his mum was a smart and diligent accountant.

One summer Sam's mum felt like she needed a break, so she and her husband decided to take a secret, late-night flight to the Amazon rainforest. They didn't tell Sam about their plan because although he was sixteen and often stayed home alone they didn't want to worry him, so they wrote him a lovely letter and made sure the fridge was stocked. The next morning, Sam woke up to an eerie silence. The house felt empty. He searched every room but couldn't find his parents. Panic started to fill his heart, so he quickly called the police.

While he waited for them to visit he found his parents' letter which had fallen off the noticeboard behind the kitchen bin. He called the police back to tell them it was all okay, only for them to tell him the grave news that his parents' plane had crashed in the dense, wild jungle of the Amazon.

Sam felt his world shatter.

The police came later that day to collect Sam and all his belongings and take him to Southampton Orphanage, a scary and nerve-wracking idea. The journey took an hour, and Sam felt sick and scared the whole way.

When they arrived at the orphanage he saw children staring out at him from what seemed like every window. Inside, a cheerful-looking nun guided him up the creaky stairs to a small, pokey but brightly lit room.

After the nun left, Sam slowly unpacked his things, folding them neatly into his drawers. Then overwhelmed with loneliness, he sat on the bed and cried until his tears ran dry.
Later, the kindly nun came up to call him down for dinner. She saw he had been crying and without saying a word, she wrapped him in a warm, tight hug that made him feel safe for the first time that day.
As they walked slowly downstairs side by side, a rich aroma reached their nostrils. The dining room was filled with happy, laughing children tucking into great bowls of soup. Sitting down to join them, Sam found the warmth of the creamy tomato soup melted away some of his sadness.
Over the next few weeks, Sam gradually settled into the routine of the orphanage and even found himself smiling and joining in their games from time to time, but the deep emptiness inside remained. He asked if there was any way he could visit the Amazon for himself to say goodbye to his parents. A kindly social worker called Susan with a warm smile and gentle eyes offered to take him.
It was steamy and hot in the jungle and millions of creepy crawlies and bugs threatened to invade their tent, but the beauty of the surroundings and the starry night sky helped to bring Sam a sense of peace. They talked to the local police and villagers about the plane crash, trying to find out if anyone knew anything, but were told over and over again how impenetrable the jungle was, and how the crash site was likely to never be found.
Despite this, Sam still had a feeling deep inside that they were somehow still out there, alive and lost. He convinced Susan to hire a guide and go searching for just one day so that he could tell himself he had done everything he could.

Despite the sun beginning to set, and their legs burning from hours of walking, Sam refused to go back. Dilly the guide and Susan insisted they turn around but Sam ran off ahead and hid behind a tree weeping, allowing himself to finally let go. In the pain of the silence that followed, he noticed a different type of noise, like the low hum of an engine. It seemed so out of place that he found himself robotically drawn towards it.

In a clearing, laid out before him was a half-destroyed plane. Inside, he came across a man, covered in dirt, and crouched over a small fan. Despite the fragile-looking body and haunted eyes, Sam knew straight away it was his father. He rushed over calling, "Dad, Dad, *Daddy!*" They hugged like they had never hugged before, gently weeping onto each other's shoulders. After what seemed like hours, Sam asked, "Where's Mum?"

His dad paused and choked out, "I don't know..."

Abigail O'Dornan (9)

The Shed

On a dark, stormy night, the thunder roared like a lion. As I walked through the narrow path that led to the darkest forest, I could feel the wind whistle around my bare head. I wish I hadn't taken this path but I had to.

Quickly, the forest appeared and my heart bounced at the thought of what was there. In the distance, the piercing light was calling me closer. Closer I stepped and found it was a black... shed.

Nervously, I pushed the creaky door open and saw a black figure sitting on the cold bed. "Hello. Who are you?" I whispered bravely.

"Come closer!" it replied in a croaky, deep voice.

I tried so hard to step closer as it demanded but my legs took me in the other direction and I ran for my life.

Just as I thought I had escaped the black figure, above me screamed the creature, "Come back!"

It was then I fell into an eternal sleep in the lonely, cold bed in the black shed of the forbidden forest.

George James Smith (9)

Chester The Hamster

Once upon a time in a small pet shop, there lived a curious hamster named Chester. He was unlike any other hamster in the shop. While his cage mates were content with their daily routine of eating, sleeping and running on their wheels, Chester yearned for adventure.

Every night, while the other hamsters snuggled into their fluffy bedding, Chester would gaze through the bars of his cage with wide, eager eyes. He dreamt of the world beyond the pet shop, of vast landscapes to explore and mysteries to unravel. And so, one fateful night, Chester made up his mind to embark on an adventure, no matter what the risks.

As the moon rose high in the sky and the shop fell silent, Chester set his plan in motion. With nimble paws and a heart full of courage, he climbed out of his cage and onto the shop floor. The world outside his cage was both thrilling and terrifying, but Chester was determined to see it all.

His first obstacles were the towering shelves that lined the shop. Undeterred, Chester scurried up the wooden shelves, his tiny claws gripping the rough surface with determination. After what felt like an eternity of climbing, he reached the top and gazed down at the shop below. The sight took his breath away. From his vantage point, Chester could see rows of colourful toys, bags of pet food and glass tanks filled with fish and reptiles. But beyond the confines of the shop, through the glass windows lay a world of endless possibilities. The streets were empty, bathed in the soft glow of streetlights, inviting Chester to step outside and explore. Without hesitation, Chester descended from the shelves and made his way towards the window. With a swift push of his tiny paws, he managed to open a small gap in the windowpane. The cool night air caressed his fur as he squeezed through the opening and landed on the sidewalk outside. The world was vast and unfamiliar. The sounds of the night, the chirping of the crickets, the whisper of the wind through the trees surrounded Chester, filling him with a mixture of excitement and apprehension. He refused to let fear hold him back. With a determined squeak, Chester set off into the unknown.

His first stop was a park nearby, where the tall grass swayed in the gentle breeze and fireflies danced in the darkness. Chester explored every nook and cranny, his whiskers twitching with curiosity as he discovered the new sights and smells. He made friends with a family of squirrels, shared stories with a wise old owl and even helped a lost ladybug find her way home.

As the night wore on, Chester's adventure took him through alleys and streets, across bridges and into hidden corners of the city. He encountered challenges along the way: a sudden rainshower, a menacing alley cat and even a narrow escape from a passing bicycle, but his spirit remained unbroken.

With each new experience, Chester grew bolder and more confident. He learned to trust his instincts, to rely on his wits and to embrace the unknown with open arms. And as the first light of dawn painted the sky in shades of pink and gold, Chester found himself at the edge of the city, looking out at the horizon stretching before him. The world was vast and full of wonders,

and Chester knew that his adventure was far from over. With a heart full of gratitude for the night that had led him there, he turned back towards the pet shop, his tiny feet carrying him home with a newfound sense of purpose.

As the sun rose on a new day, Chester slipped back into his cage, his fur ruffled and his eyes sparkling with the memory of his grand adventure. The other hamsters watched in awe as he settled into his bedding, a fearless explorer returned from a journey beyond their wildest dreams. And, as Chester closed his eyes and drifted off to sleep, he knew that the night had changed him forever. He was no longer just a hamster in a pet shop; he was Chester, the adventurer, the dreamer, the brave soul who dared to step into the unknown and discover the magic that lay beyond.

Jasmine Carbaugh (11)

Sitting In The Dark

S itting in the dark
I n silence
T he eerie silence
T alking to the lurking shadows
I n my dim room
N o one else in my dim room
G hostly things happen in the dark, in silence.

I feel the ice-cold, biting breeze
N owhere to shelter from the ice-cold, biting breeze, like the whisper of a ghost in the room.

T he dark is a bad place to sit but still
H olding onto myself tightly, I sit in the dark
E eriness waits and watches as I sit in the dark in my dim room.

D ust is slowly and freely wafting around me in the darkness
A flock of dust wafting in the darkness
R ound and round go the shadows turning me delirious like kites in the wind
K ites flying around in my dim room as I'm sitting in the dark.

Dilys Hall

Emma And The Disasters

My name is Emma and I'm writing a story about a terrifying experience that made me and my family traumatised till this very day, an experience that cost the lives of millions of animals and humans.
On August 8 2031, I was alone with my two annoying sisters. Our mother sent us to get food and water. As we went to the corner shop we heard a rumble on the ground. My sisters and I were astonished and curious to find out what it was, we saw cracks everywhere.
The cracks came closer and closer to us and made a ring shape around us, the floor beneath us cracked and tumbled down. I grabbed on the edge and told them to grab my hand. Thankfully, we made it out safely but this was only the start of the disaster.
We saw something even more terrifying... a tornado, not so far transforming. I grabbed my sister's hands and ran as fast as I could. I saw my building. As I got there I heard people screaming. I was sure that this was the beginning of a new stage of the Earth, the Ice Stage. It was impossible but now it was possible.
I got to the apartment, and my mother, who was in her chair, pointed at the window. I and my sisters saw a huge wave as tall as a mountain. It was heading our way. My mother told us to leave without her but I wasn't ready to leave her there, because there was so much we hadn't explored in the world. Then she said there was a place that was safe for as to go to. It was called The Survives.
I packed our things so quickly I didn't notice that our suitcase was almost full. We ran to the check point as fast as we could. We saw a person arguing with the security

guard. I heard them arguing about not letting the dog in and then he got kicked out. My sisters and I were next in line, we were shocked that it was for free to enter. We rushed in and later saw a guard guiding us to our beds. We slept and felt a big push by the time we woke up.

The guard told us that we were in Asia. I used to be in LA but now I'm in Asia The person jumped out. We looked out of the window, what we saw was so terrifying it almost made my soul jump out of my body. It explained why I saw people running in the other direction. It was a massive... a giant terrifying hurricane was heading our way.

I woke up my sisters and grabbed both of their hands. Our guide showed us a transport tube that would take us to the nearest continent. We made it to this place in Africa called Ghana and we stayed for the night. It was very hard to sleep in the night.

We woke up the next morning but it wasn't daylight that we saw, it was the gigantic hurricane again. I told my sisters to wake up but one of them didn't make it in time and I saw her die.

The guide told us to hurry inside the transport pods and we made it to Antarctica. I saw a group of people and I went to them with my last sister, who was still in tears. I felt so bad for her. She hadn't slept or eaten since our sister died. She hadn't been the same. We heard a crackling sound beneath the surface. Then a massive spaceship came, and a Navy guard came out of it. He said, "Get on, Emma and Isabella." I didn't know who this man was but everyone was coming on the ship so I also followed along with my sister. I got aboard and the guy said, "Welcome my daughters!"

I realised it was Dad. I'd made it out safely with my sister. Now I'm 26 and I have a husband and 2 kids. As for Isabela, she has an important job to search for a new planet that is habitable for humans.

Isata Kamara (9)

Ben's Pizza-Eater

Twenty years into the future, Sir Ben had a bright idea to start his own business where everything was just 1p! So cheap, right?
Every sort of pizza, drink or ice cream will come right to you in seconds, whilst you relax in the cosy outdoor pool or jacuzzi.
Pizzas come in all types and sizes with any topping you want. These may include: cheese, tomato, pepperoni, pineapple, ham, pork, bacon, sausage and even twenty-four karat *gold* (which is edible).
There are also lots of ice cream flavours to choose from, which may consist of: strawberry, chocolate, vanilla, bubblegum, mint, lemon, gold flakes, flakes and much more. There are lots of toppings to put on it as well like sauces, sprinkles or flakes. Remember, everything costs 1p!
How about rating us on Pizza Adviser? Five stars? So please come to Ben's Pizza-Eater. Entry costs are free.

Ben Dinh (9)

The Spirit Story

One dark night, there was a girl called Jacky. She was sound asleep until... *Thump, thump, thump, thump.* She woke up, so she started to try to wake her parents up, but they would not wake up until... *Clash, bam.* Her heart stopped. Her parents were almost under a spell.
Courageously she went downstairs and saw a gigantic mess. "Who could have done this?" Jacky said. Then she saw footprints leading to the garden. Lila and Mila, Jacky's cat and dog, were also in a deep sleep. Tiredly, she sloped up the stairs, locked her room, and jumped into bed.
"*Argh!*" said Mum. "What happened?"
"Oh no," said Dad.
Jacky was still in her room, but she felt a shiver. Her room was unlocked, and footprints were leading into her room. Mum and Dad came bursting into the room. "Are you okay?" asked Dad.
"Did you do this?" asked Mum.
Jacky said no. Jacky started to get worried. "Oh look, Lila and Mila." But she started thinking about Grandma Ryla who passed because of cancer, even though Mum and Dad did not care because of an argument they had. As she peered into the garden, she found a note saying: 'I will not hurt you, just your parents who did not care about me.' Hours later, Jacky got tired of not asking her parents why they did not care about Ryla, so she ran upstairs like a lightning bolt. She asked her parents, and they said they had to leave her, and they had a discussion, and she was left alone.

Then Grandpa Rack came and she thought she was happy again. "*What?* How can someone be okay being left alone?" Two days later, she still held a grudge against her parents. She had an idea. As she thought of it, she started to get hungry.
"*Dinner is ready!*" shouted Mum.
"Thank goodness," Jacky said hungrily.
The next day, she cooked Grandma's favourite dish, spicy curry and fresh lemonade. Jacky was only thirteen, and she was doing well after she cooked. She fed Lila and Mila.
It was night. Jacky snuck into the garden until... "*Meow!*"
"Woah!" Jacky screamed in terror.
"*Meow!*"
Jacky said, "*Lila?* You scared me." She ran up the stairs.
"What? Who? My drawing is scribbled." It was a drawing of her parents, and she had noticed that the mess only happened at night, so there would be a big mess.
The next day, the food that she made was wiped clean. The mess was not so messy, but it had been eight days of cleaning.
The next day at night, she felt the spirit. "Grandma?" She showed herself. Jacky had a flood of tears in her eyes seeing Grandma for the first time. She hugged her, but she was pale, and she looked sad.
She ran into her room. She felt sad until her dad came into her room and said, "Grandpa is coming for a week." It was time to explain all the mess that had been happening, and she explained everything. They believed her.
"*Grandpa is here!*" Jacky gave Grandpa Rack a hug. Rack also brought her eighteen and nineteen-year-old brother and sister. Jacky explained everything.

It was night. All of a sudden, they saw the spirit, and they all hugged her. She smiled and said she was at peace. She flew into the sky, and they all started crying.

Joycie Arcos (10)

This Is Me

My name is Mehdi Ali and I'm not that tall
I'm an average height, not too small
Whenever I'm upset, gloomy or sad
My friends cheer me up and it's not so bad.

I've got brown skin
I'm not that fat, I'm quite thin
I like to play football
I do boxing but I don't like to brawl.

I like to watch television
I like maths but I'm not good at division
I have a cute baby brother
I have a dad, sister and mother.

My favourite snake is a cobra snake
My favourite dessert is probably cake
One of my best friends is Cecil
However, sometimes he's a pain in a... vessel.

I'm quite fast, like a cheetah
If I am in a race I will probably beat ya
One of my friends who is faster than me is Adam
He once told me he is a madman.

Mehdi-Ali Shah

My Own Unicorn: Elizabeth And The Defeat Of The Monster

I was on my way to school when I tripped over a rock and fell in a hole, down, down, down. I fell and hit my head, closing my eyes because my head really hurt.
In a few minutes, I woke up. Suddenly I discovered I was in an *enchanted forest!* I hoped there were unicorns because I'd always loved unicorns.
I was scared, looking left and right till I bumped into a... *unicorn!* I... was... astonished. Then I jumped up and down, I was super happy.
When I was thinking about keeping my own unicorn, suddenly, before I knew it, I was on the unicorn's back flying. I was so scared, I thought I would slip off and fall but no, I didn't.
Soon I thought of a name, I named it... *Elizabeth!* What a cute name. Then, Elizabeth landed on the moon. We sat there. She was so cute. I knew she was going to be mine and when I first saw that unicorn, I knew at the end I might take her home and introduce her to my mum and dad. By the way, this is where the crazy story starts.
I was feeling really sleepy so I closed my eyes and slept. A few minutes later, Elizabeth shook her mane and sparkle dust came down and went on my nose. It tickled so much I had to sn-sn- *Achoo!* I woke up and guess what? I saw a group of... *unicorns!*

I said hi. Nobody replied, not one word came out. Suddenly, they were shouting and arguing but so loudly I had to cover my ears. I calmed them down by showing a picture but they were still angry and one of the unicorns ripped my picture apart. I put a lot of time into that, I was really upset.
When I wiped my tears, everyone was gone apart from Elizabeth then I saw my familiar monster from my fairytale book. That meant... the defeat of the monster!
I was so scared but I had to use my memories to defeat the monster. The first step was to find the sword, the second step was to get the sword out of the rock and lastly, the third step was to slice the monster's eye.
I told Elizabeth the unicorn to distract the monster, then I was looking for the sword when I found it. It was behind the monster. I ran towards the sword and tried pulling it. "*Argh! I did it!*"
Elizabeth was getting tired. I said, "Just a little more." She did all she could while I was climbing up.
I climbed up but I was slipping off but I had an idea. I told Elizabeth to fly me and land me on the monster's face. She took me there and... I sliced the monster's eye off.
All the unicorns came back and cheered on for me, "*Hooray!*" I saved the day.
I saw a portal. I thought, *it'll take me home.* I took my unicorn with me but it wouldn't let her. I said bye, I gave her a big hug and went to the portal.
I landed home. Mum was worried, she said, "Where have you been?"
I thought of an idea. "At the park with my friends," I said with a giggle.

The next day we had a test but I remembered Elizabeth so I mistakenly wrote 'unicorn' on my test. I got zero out of thirty, *whoops!* Mum wasn't impressed, me neither.
I had a unicorn dream, it was me and Elizabeth. The next day was a unicorn party at the weekend. I wished Elizabeth was there.

Fidelity Matthew (9)

Euro Football Game

The month of May came,
The beginning of the Euro game.
England, Poland, France,
All countries had a chance.
I sat down in front of the TV every night
And invited my friends if they were polite.
Each team ran fast on the field
And because of this many goals were achieved.
Day after day, football games,
Every day someone went away.
I carefully recorded every score
Because I expected my favourite team to win more.

The day of the final came,
England against Spain!
Every house in the neighbourhood waited,
The flag of England was waved!
The first and second goals - everyone was shouting for joy,
And we waited to start to enjoy.
But unfortunately it was the final whistle,
Spain started to bristle!
All of Spain was now celebrating
With the Euro 2024 Cup waving!

Nikola Ivanov (8)

The Journey Back In Time

I was complaining to my mom one day that I couldn't have my phone or iPad with dinner. She responded by saying, "You have devices with dinner all week but on a Sunday we are going to start eating together and talking to each other around the table."

I was horrified! My parents began trying to make conversation with my younger sister. As I was feeling bored my eyes wandered to the window. There I saw in the night sky a shooting star. In my head I wished, *please take me back to where I will be happy again.* I wish I had been specific with my wish because I ended up on a farm... Where was I and where was my family?

I saw a small cottage-looking house nearby so I hurried over and knocked on the door. A lady answered in some farm outfit. I said, "Hi, I'm kind of lost, can I use your mobile to call my mom please?"

The lady looked at me strange. "A mobile? What's that?" she asked.

"A phone," I answered with a strange look on my face.

"No, we can't afford phones round here," she said. "I must say your clothes are rather strange," she added.

"*What?* This is a designer tracksuit! It's Nike!" I explained.

The lady frowned at me and said, "Well there's a police station up the road but they're not open yet, you can play with my kids till it is." She pointed to a few paces away where I saw nine children.

I approached them. "Erm... hi, your mom said I could play with you guys for a bit. I'm Athena," I explained.

"These are my brothers and sisters but the only name you need to remember right now is mine. I'm Kathleen, Kathleen Trimble," said one of the girls. I was in complete shock! Kathleen Trimble was my nan! Had I gone back in time? I had to be sure.
I asked her all the names of her brothers, sisters and her parents and my theory was correct - it was my family. I didn't want to freak them out so I said nothing about it, I just played with them. There were no phones or consoles, there was only one small television with a few channels - and it was black and white! There weren't loads of toys or snacks but before I had the chance to freak out, the children asked me to play.
I actually had fun playing outside, running around in the sun, breathing in the fresh air, thinking of games to invent and play. I loved seeing the animals. I got to know my family a lot better without all the distractions my reality provided. Later, I sat around the dinner table and we all spoke of our day, then Kathleen offered to take me to the police station. It was a little dark outside. I stopped for a second to look at the stars - something I never noticed in my own reality before. That's when I realised what my parents were trying to do for me by taking my phone. I saw another shooting star and wished to go back home to my time.
It worked, I was back home and it was just before dinner. Before Mom could even suggest a technology-free dinner I suggested it myself. She was in shock but very pleased. From then on I tried to have a healthy balance of technology and reality.

Athena Pointon (11)

The Lifeless Alleyway

It was midnight. I was running, heart pacing trying to escape the loud footsteps that were stomping behind me. The mysterious figure was breaking everything it passed. I came up to the end of the alleyway and all I could hear at that point was a slow gasping breath slowly whispering three simple words repeatedly. "Please don't leave."
I ran all the way through the cobbled streets, past the closed shops, and through my front door, until all I could feel was warmth and a pleasant cosy feeling. I thought of what had happened, I considered who the mysterious figure could be. If it really didn't want me to leave, then it would have used force to stop me from its terrifying grasp.
The next day, I walked past the same alleyway on my way to work. The eerie feeling coming out of it pulled me in like a magnet. Before I knew it, I was walking through the same creepy alleyway that I had run from the night before. I heard footsteps, loud footsteps, and at that moment, I realised that it was the same person as before. Only this time, I didn't run. I walked slowly and calmly and waited for the person to do what they wanted.
I heard a small voice say, "You came back!" At that moment, two adults came into the dim light, each with a small child in their arms. They were all covered in dirt, and the lady looked as though she was going to collapse. My instincts immediately kicked in, and I rushed forward to help them both. I guided the whole lot back to my home and settled them in before I did anything.
After a long chat with the family, I started realising their position. They used to live in the countryside with a lot of their relatives until one night, gang members showed up at their house and asked the grandparents for all their money.

When they refused, they were shot, and the gang members made the rest of them an offer. The lady was trembling as she told me that they had to give the gang fifty pounds every five days or they would all get beat up and they couldn't contact the authorities or else. A wave of pity washed over me. I stared at the family and thought of everything I could do. I sent them off to sleep and sat in my bed staring into space.

The next morning, I gave the family fifty pounds and told them that I would return in less than four hours. As soon as they were out of my sight, I sprinted to the police station and told the police officers everything. The police crept up the alleyway and launched themselves at the gang, but while all this was happening, I realised the family weren't making any noise. The police split up at last and on the ground, I saw two adults and two babies lying lifeless on the ground.

Amna Athar (11)

Misleading Mien

Last winter will be forever etched in my memory, for I learned how appearances can be extremely deceptive! As a blanket of fear enveloped me, I - the new girl at Oakwood Primary School - stood shivering in the icy cold wind. From behind me a burly boy, of about thirteen years old, strongly kicked my skinny, spindly legs, which caused my gaunt body to topple over and end up head-first into a colossal pile of mud. Through my clotted-with-mud ears, I could hear jeering, mocking children, showering insults at me. Closing my droopy eyelids, like I was blind, I felt my way through the spiky, tall altitude entrance doors, as if they were gritting their jaws menacingly at me.
Standing motionlessly in the deserted playground, waiting for the bell to ring, bitter rain tumbled continuously down my pale countenance and drenched my scruffy school uniform. Up above in the gloomy sky, melancholic, slate-grey clouds drifted across the sky malevolently as if they were waiting for me.
When no bell was heard, fear struck me. Racing through multiple rooms, I finally found my Year Five class through the maze of corridors. Breathlessly, I creaked open the door as quietly as I could, but the swarm of huge heads towards me instantly as I cowered down to a corner.
"Why on Earth are you late?" demanded the teacher with an enormous frown and large fists held up high, clear enough for everyone to see.
"I didn't hear the bell," I mumbled, almost in tears.

"Sit down immediately!" exclaimed Mr Rage, his face reddening. Staring around for any empty seats, I knew exactly where to sit - right at the back of the class. Rushing towards my seat, I sighed deeply, wishing it would swallow me up.

"Ay you, new kid, where you from?" jeered Sally sarcastically. Following a deafening silence, Sally screamed, "Not answering ay? You just wait till break!"

Suddenly the break bell rang and a bolt of fear shot through my starving stomach. The dreaded time had come. With one word that Sally uttered, she tripped on a huge tree stump in the middle of the playground. Her arm split open and litres of blood spurted everywhere. Recalling the lessons of first aid I had completed, I grabbed the medical box and began to patch up Sally.

Once the work was complete, Sally stuttered, "Thank you!" Taken aback by these kindhearted words, I accepted them politely. Walking arm in arm off the playground, hoping Sally learned a valuable lesson that day: don't judge a book by its cover.

Saanvi Upadhyaya (11)

The Queen's Knickers

One day Jasmine went to collect the post. She brought it back to her lovely, sweet, welcoming home. She went to the garden where her family was and read the letter out loud. She said, "'Dear family, this letter contains four tickets and is inviting you to see the Queen. Pick carefully. Be at my castle at 12pm. Give my soldiers your tickets and they will let you in. From the Queen.'"
"OMG, we get to see the *Queen! Ahhh!*" said Emelie.
"Mum, can we get boba please?" said Jasmine.
"No is the answer," said Jade, "we need to get ready to see the Queen in a few hours."
"I found a really cute outfit, Jasmine," said Emelie.
"That's beautiful, do you wanna see mine?" said Jasmine.
"Sure," said Emelie, "it's gorgeous."
"Here we are. It's massive! Stay with me so you don't get lost. Here's the tickets, sir," said Jade.
"Hello Your Majesty," said the family at the same time.
"Let's say our ages, youngest to oldest."
"Four."
"Eight."
"Thirty-one."
"Thirty-eight."
"Ninety-three."
"Let's go and have food. It's so golden," said the Queen.
What do you mean golden? Jasmine thought.
"We were eating it?" said Cass.

100

"Oh no, this is for display only. I will tape it shut in a room till the end. The royal family is waiting to see you all in the royal sitting room," said the Queen. "Now nobody knows anyone's name so let's say our names from the youngest person to oldest. Other family first."
"Emelie."
"Jasmine."
"Jade."
"Cass."
"Now the royal family."
"Jacob."
"Lance."
"Lacy."
"The Queen."
"The King."
"Okay, now let's go to the gold room," said the Queen.
"There's a thief chase," said Cass.
"But I need to go toilet," said the Queen. "*OMG, my knickers are gone and I am locked in the toilet!*"
"I will save you," said Cass. "Oooh, doughnuts, bye!"
Finally Jade helped.

Jasmine Cumberbatch (7)

Respect

Nearly anything can earn you *respect* in the eyes of others. But only certain things can earn you respect in the eyes of those who are respected.
It's that simple.
So true respect is not earned by breaking the law or injuring oneself.
The respect earned by that is not true and lasting, it *will* be reaffirmed.
It is *so important* for some to be respected that they would do the same to elders and parents.
However, the way to earn respect is to be respectful, not a thing after being given to someone to prove to themselves that they can be respectful.
It has to occur pure and naturally.
It can not be demolished by anything or anyone, therefore, respect is something that people would do anything for.
Some might die or some can also endure endless pain and suffering if they think others can respect them for it.
It is absolutely ridiculous and poor if anyone can't respect you for who you truly are.
This doesn't mean to earn others' respect, it just slowly means to love them even if they don't respect you.
Some can think that others can respect themselves so why do we have to respect them but no.
To me, respect means that you listen to someone's ideas and thoughts, follow rules that have been established.
To respect someone is not to assume they are invisible but to notice that they are a human being too trying to search for traces of respect.

Most people, like me, try to depend on only freely given respect that is usually already acquired in your normal acts of manner and events with people, rather than trying to earn or impress the respect of someone.
True respect is like true love.
It is unconditional.
It is timeless.
Just like true love, it can never be taken away.
Respect for a person is always there once they acknowledge and establish it purely and honestly.
On the other hand, trust, anger, envy, hate and all the other good or bad things in the whole world can be demolished.
Respect is different than trust, it's not just a person.
It can be something genuine.
Real respect, I believe it's an attitude or an alter ego.
However, once it is given to a person, then yes... it can be destroyed.
That is real respect!

Saanvi Bolisetty (11)

Sam's Realisation

Striding down the leafy path, Sam, a brilliant businessman, was coming home after a tiring day at work. In his pockets, bank notes and cheques bulged while some just fell out. When he got home he would be greeted by his cat called Freddy, who he didn't like very much. Although he didn't particularly like work, he loved money and power.

As soon as Sam stepped into his mansion, he raced to his work desk so he could admire all of his earnings. When he had just gotten started, he felt a nudge on his leg. He looked down and saw Freddy with a toy mouse in his mouth. Sam simply pushed him away and went back to admiring his money. Freddy, who felt very lonely, went to his bed in misery. Sam was greedy - madly greedy.

Finally, after about one hour, Sam relented from looking at his earnings and went to feed Freddy. He suspected he'd be in the cat room, where his bed was, but surprisingly, as he came into the room, he saw that Freddy was nowhere to be seen. *That's weird*, he thought. It was the same in all the other rooms. He searched the living room, bathroom, kitchen and dining room but to his dismay, he couldn't see Freddy. With every passing second his worry deepened.

For hours, Sam searched and called for Freddy but it proved a challenge as he battled with guilt. What also slowed him down was the mountain of cash that he had been so obsessed with just a few hours ago. After searching for about 12 hours his heart had become a pit of misery, guilt and despair.

When he got into bed, stifling misery poured through his veins. Was this a punishment for his greediness? This was not a life worth living to Sam.

After a fitful sleep and dreams of being catless, Sam woke up bright and early. Suddenly he heard a high-pitched noise. There it was again! All of a sudden, a ball of fluff came rolling out from behind the bedpost. But from further inspection, he saw that it was Freddy! Tears of joy ran down his face and his mouth curved into a beaming smile. "I love you so much Freddy!" cried Sam. Freddy started purring madly and Sam realised how good it felt to be kind and he decided he would never again put his money over his orange feline friend Freddy.

Sidney Nicholson (10)

Stoke Bishop

Reception is all play and fun,
Where friendships are formed and done.
Two classes are practically one,
Then, ten months later you'll move on.

Year One is more serious and business-like,
Though don't let that give you a fright.
Building more knowledge you are,
Yet from Year Six you are quite far.

Year Two is where you concentrate on how to multiply,
Then this thing you will work out and simplify.
You now really get the swing of it all,
Everything you take on is super cool.

Year Three is the middle one now,
Though don't give up and frown.
Key Stage Two you have stepped up to, of course,
Trust me, this year is not forced.

Year Four you get to do a play about present and past,
Because it's extremely fun it goes fast.
News, monarchs, inventions, costs and more,
It gives you a tingly feeling in the core.

Year Five you do some nice trips I must say,
This year everything is okay.
An unforgettable, awesome year,
Though the end is very nearly here.

Year Six is the greatest of them all,
Many happy memories you can recall.
Cute little buddies by your side,
Happiness comes over you like a tide.

An incredible play you'll get to do,
Make sure to remember lines and cues.
Camp is filled up to the brim with fun,
Yet soon you'll have to pack and be done.

You get hoodies that are extremely bright,
They look so cool and right.
Work hard at SATs and it will be fine,
Remember never to say a negative line.

Sadly, I am here now to say a final and painful goodbye,
Many memories this building has carried and supplied.
Everywhere here there is hopefulness and smiles,
And of course, the friendships of which there are piles.

Never ever will I forget this beauty of a place,
Never ever could anything come and replace.
Never ever this place will buckle and fall,
Never ever a sad moment I recall.

Fall into the fun and don't look back,
Learn and flourish away and never slump and slack.
Colours line the walls of this incredible place,
All the opportunities you must embrace.

Luna Stevens (11)

Save Water

Water, water, drop by drop,
Saves every field and every crop.

Please don't put the tap on,
The hosepipe ban has ruined our lawn...

Save water when it rains,
Stop wasting water in drains...

No water for us, no water for pets,
Save the water before we regret!

Drop by drop, let's save water
Then our lives won't be harder.

Lakes, rivers, seas and oceans!
Summer holidays with fun 'n' emotions...

Sad am I, all is getting dry...
What can we do
To get this problem through?

Ah, I got a point!
So let's rewind...

Saving water every day will bring new life,
Let's create a world where we all survive.

I promise today I promise to do,
Save water every day... Will you?

Siya Bisht (9)

Ocean's Farewell

Whoosh, whoosh, whoosh. The winter breeze stroked my face as I looked around - surrounded by my favourite people, sitting in my favourite place, doing my favourite things. Was I really ready to leave it all behind?
The crickets chirped in my ear as I relished the comforting chatter of my loved ones, adjacent to the bonfire that flickered like a broken light. The waves crashed against the shore, bringing with them the gift of the beach: seashells. Different yet similar. The unique shells: some square, some circle, some brown, some white, some speckled or striped. Each unique. Once again, I found myself hypnotised by the serenity of the beach. The cliffs stood high and proud - protective like a mother to its child. The ocean - teal and clear, welcoming with waves of invitations to enter its waters.
Enjoying the mere beauty of my environment, I tasted warm, perfectly toasted clouds of sugar - marshmallows. Pink and white, just like when I was a kid; when the beach wasn't forgotten, when people cared more about experiences of life than materialistic things. Oh, how I missed those times.
The crackle of the fire brought me back to the present - it was my last day here - I needed to enjoy it. As I gazed at what lay in front of me, I felt the warmth of the bonfire embracing me like apricity. The golden, gorgeous and grainy sand rubbed against my feet as I shuffled, confused by the bittersweet experience. Staring into the fire, I was reminded of the flames of ambitions I once possessed.
Soon enough, it was sunset. The gradient of blue to pink to orange were chapters of life. All different. Yet coming together to form something mesmerising.

Ready to leave, I got up saying final goodbyes. Paralysed once more by the magnificent and magical scene, I stood on the cliff smelling the salty water, admiring nature and a feeling of utter and pure gratitude took over me -knowing that my last day on my beautiful planet was better than anything I could've asked for. My eyes welled up with tears as I felt the breeze stroke my face... One last time.

Aalisha Tyagi (11)

Spooky Cave

In a cave were spiders and darkness. It was near London. It was called the Spooky Cave or Haunted Cave. No one ever went there.

One day a boy went in there. Nothing was there. Another person ran in. The door shut and everything got locked. The boy got a letter saying 'I am here and I see you.' The two boys were scared. They heard a voice saying, "I can smell you. Come up." There was a loud scream saying, "I see you now, *come upstairs!*"

The boys saw a creepy smile on the wall. Everywhere they looked, they saw the face. They went close and hit the wall. The face, smiling, turned red. This meant that they had to run as far as possible.

They both ran with all their speed, hitting the smiling face again. It turned sad. He saw a hammer. He smashed it on the wall. A note said 'Come and smile with me.' But they did not smile.

They went into a room. They saw the boss. He was controlling the smiles. He chased them. He had tubes that turned people into bones. When he stopped they touched him. He made a button and then all the faces came everywhere.

The boss had a key and gave it to his friend while he went up. He was running and all the faces were coming. He attacked them all and saw the boss. The boss was mad and tried to get the boy. The boy ran on the ladder. The boss said, "I will get you."

The kid said, "No you cannot. I am fast." He ran and got a big stick of wood and set it on fire, using the stick his father gave him.

The boss was shocked. He said, "I will get *you!*" The boy got two ropes and logs and glued them and made a ladder. He ran up.
The next day he woke and the boy he saw was his brother. Then he ran to the cave and started breaking it to pieces. It was a rock called flint. Flint could make fire. The monster ran and all the smiles ran. The monster was having mini monsters everywhere. We might not know who was the monster. And only we know the boy went into the cave. No one else went into the spooky cave. The flint was for a camping shop.

Akshayan Vivekanantharajah (8)

The Missing But Not Seen

It all started when we set off to a lovely lively place we all went to as kids. Even my mum would tell me stories about how amazing and joyful Spain was. We always went to the beautiful beaches and hotels in the safe areas of Spain and had tour guides with us for safety but one day we said to the tour guide we were okay for the day. We were only going to a nearby restaurant which was only a mile away. It had many tourists and kind people so we weren't really expecting anything to happen.

We had a few drinks in a nearby bar first and then went to a beautiful restaurant for some pasta salad dishes which were lovely. We had a few drinks each and even tipped the lovely waitress for her brilliant service. We got up and walked off. Suddenly, we were stopped by a man selling some watches at the side of the ginnel. We looked and declined. We walked off towards the town as it was early. But I still felt as if the man who was selling those items was following us. We tried to dodge him by going down some side streets but what we didn't expect was a kidnap ring of gangsters owning the house at the end of the back ginnel.

We spotted something we shouldn't have seen... a man was being put into the boot of a car and drove off pretty fast. We tried to sneakily run off to avoid them but the dark-haired man saw us and started to chase us.

At this point, we were all panicking and getting worried. What should we do? Trying to catch our breath from running so much, we were lost in the middle of nowhere. My friend needed his meds. This was a disaster. There was no police about and we had no cash. If we went back the way we came were the bad men who were after us going to kill

us? What are we going to do? We had no way of communicating. We were all tired, lost, scared and freaked out.
We tried to make a plan to get back to the hotel for our things. Suddenly, we heard a sound. Oh no! It was him. He had brought more men with him. They parked up looking around. It was the same car as before.

Jacob Rawlinson (10)

Rose In Astoria

On a warm, sunny afternoon, a kind, shy girl named Rose was baking cookies with her helpful mother. Once they had finished their cookies, Rose decided to take some cookies to the animals in the large, majestic forest next to her house. She skipped happily to the forest and started to walk back home but she stopped in her tracks. She saw a bright, blue glow in the distance. She realised it was a magic portal! She edged closer to this mysterious portal wondering where it led to.

Rose jumped through the portal with bravery hoping she made the right decision. When she opened her eyes, she found that she was in a magical land! There were clouds made of cotton candy and rainbows as far as the eye could see. Unicorns were flying, mermaids were swimming and dragons were sleeping. It was like she was in a world that she had created herself. Rose was astonished!

She then saw a pink glow at the top of a tall, grey mountain. She wondered what it was, so she began to climb the mountain. When Rose got halfway, there were a pile of massive stones blocking her way up the mountain and a beautiful unicorn flew over to Rose with great pride. She moved the stones out of the way with her wings and did it with great strength. Rose thanked the unicorn and she flew away into the sunset. Rose carried on climbing and didn't look back.

Rose finally got to the top and she was exhausted. She now knew what the pink glow was, it was a wishing crystal as bright as the sun! With these crystals, you could wish for anything you liked and it would come true. Rose wished to go back home to her mother and her sister Ruby.

She closed her eyes and when she opened them, she was in her kitchen and to her surprise, it was like nothing had happened! Rose was confused, but she told her mother and sister all about her adventure in Astoria and all of the wonderful things that she had done with great excitement while they listened in amazement.

Lexi Warrington (9)

The Long-Lost Secret

For as long as I'd known, I'd been alone in the woods. Abandoned, at the age of four... No family at all. Just one small picture of strangers, who abandoned me. Left me, all alone. Why? I didn't know. It didn't matter now, my home was in the woods. I was used to it. Nature, animals, peace, it was great.

Eventually, once in a while a child came roaming into the woods, they never lasted. Although, one stood out, a girl, who went by the name of Emma. Features so distinct, so similar. We instantly got along, it was so unconventional. I always wondered what it would be like to see my sister, she reminded me so much of her. I know, it's silly but although I didn't remember much, it felt like I knew so much.

She came by the woods every morning, we played, laughed, and messed about. However, sometimes she attempted to sneak in some questions about me, about my life and family, which I was unsure, uncomfortable about but she always shared empathy.

It came time. She begged over and over for me to come over, explore the city, her house, and see her family. It took me a while to comprehend this, making me feel anxious, strange. Eventually, I agreed.

One morning she came by, her emotions shining so bright. We walked and walked and walked. Then, we were so worn out, she decided to show me her house, her family. I walked in through the door frame and froze. The picture. It was the same one they had hung in the entry. Tears filled my eyes. I barraged Emma with questions, I wanted answers. I needed them.

Her mum, she walked in. She knew, I saw it in her eyes. Me and Emma, we were sisters. They abandoned me. I confronted her, as she fled to the ground, in disbelief. In disappointment of herself.
"I thought, I thought my sister passed away, that's what you told me, Mum!" Emma exclaimed, confused.
Years later... it changed, life did, family did. Everything changed...

Lena Saif (8)

Good And Evil

All our life we are told the difference between a bad person and a good person, good and evil. But what if I told you the only difference is who tells the story?

When we look around the world what do we see? Sure, we see some questionable people who sometimes lead questionable lives. Yes, most of the time it's just someone with a weird life and they have no reasonable motive, but that small percentage of people have good reasons. The idea of something not being inherently bad with good intentions is known as deontological ethics, an example being that someone might have stolen. Now, on its own that's bad, right? But what if they did it to save their starving family? What if they had no other choice? Thinking of whether still being good or okay is deontological ethics. On the other side, we have the reverse. What if somebody did something good like donate £1,000 to charity for more fame? Now, if you just heard that they donated £1,000 to charity, well, that's good. But when you hear they did it for personal gain, well, it's kind of selfish in a way. They don't care for the people they give to and selfishness is a trait of a bad person.

You may be thinking, what has this got to do with our starting statement? Well, it's news things circulating. You may see something on TV, for example: "Breaking news, local resident Emma Shropford stole children's clothes from Next for reasons unknown." You may think that's bad. Then later that day your friend may tell you that same story with the reason why, being she was poor and in need of clothes for her children. Hearing that someone risked jail time for

her children, you may think that's good. Two of the same stories but different reasons. In one, Emma is pictured as bad, the other as good.
And that is why you shouldn't judge because you don't always know the full story.

Athena Smith (11)

Heartbreak And Glory

29th December 2022. Lusail Stadium, Qatar. Argentina versus France in the FIFA World Cup Final. This was a match to be remembered for the ages.

And it only took twenty-three minutes for Argentina to take the lead, when Lionel Messi, considered by many to be the GOAT (AKA Greatest Of All Time) of football, scored from the penalty spot after a foul on his beloved teammate Ángel Di Maria, and the latter would eventually make it 2-0. This would only add to Les Bleus' miseries. And you would be forgiven for thinking that the thirty-sixth-minute goal was the final nail in the coffin. Oh, how wrong you would be.

In both the eightieth and eighty-first minutes, Kylian Mbappé (then a legend for PSG) scored, the first with a penalty after Randal Kolo Muani was fouled and the second a wonderful finish after a pass from Marcus Thuram.

In extra time, Argentina would again take the lead through a goal from Messi through the barest of margins, after it was very nearly found to have cleared off the line after it went in, and a very close onside decision. But French hero Mbappé scored another penalty after a handball from Gonzalo Montiel in the eighteen-yard box. This ensured that penalties were coming, and they did indeed come.

Emiliano Martínez got in the minds of Kingsley Coman and Aurélien Tchouameni, whose penalties had been saved and missed respectively. Then, Montiel, the man who conceded France's second penalty of the game, stepped up. The tension was all on him to see if he would score or if Hugo Lloris would make a miracle.

And score he did!

Argentina were champions for the third time. As Kylian Mbappé stared in disbelief at what would've been, Messi and his team celebrated as Messi could finally complete his trophy cabinet. Heartbreak on one side, yet glory on the other.

Yatharth Rangineni (12)

The Adventures Of Horsley The Tiger

One sunny morning, Horsley the Tiger decided to take his class on a field trip to the jungle. Horsley the Tiger reminded his class to take with them their drinks, snacks and their coats. The little tigers all lined up and climbed onto the bus. As the bus started to leave, the little tigers all began to sing songs. Their favourite song was Cotton Eye Joe. The journey was long and it began to rain.

When they arrived at the jungle, they were amazed at the ginormous jungle. Horsley the Tiger began to lead the class into the jungle and they looked at the tall trees, the baby dinosaurs and lots of kangaroos.

Horsley the Tiger could not help feeling like they were being watched. Horsley the Tiger began to look at the shadows. The shadows changed shape to shape. The little tigers began to get scared and Horsley the Tiger tried to be brave and scare the shadow away. Out of the shadows stepped a baby T-rex who was crying. The baby T-rex was crying because it had lost its family.

The little tigers wanted to help the baby T-rex. They all began to look all around. All of a sudden, they heard a noise. The noise they heard was a loud roaring noise and the ground began to shake. Out of the trees appeared a giant mummy T-rex and a giant daddy T-rex. When they saw the baby T-rex they said, "Thank you for finding our baby." Just then Horsley the Tiger heard another growl. This time the growl came from the mummy and daddy T-rexes' tummies. Baby Rex said, "We're hungry." Mummy T-rex asked the class whether they would like to come for tea.

Horsley the Tiger looked at their own rumbling bellies and said they had to get back.

Horsley the Tiger began to take the class back to the bus when they heard a loud ringing noise. Suddenly Horsley the Tiger sat up and looked around. He then realised it was just a dream.

Evaline Lewak (8)

A Little Cottage By A Stream

I live in a cottage, a little cottage by a stream. I live with my mama and papa and my sister, my little sister Mary. Sometimes I think, I think to myself how wonderful it would be to have a brother, a little brother. I used to have a brother, a little brother but... he... died... that's why we live here. In a cottage, a little cottage by a stream. I love it here just... us. So did my brother, my little brother but... he... died. Mama said we are moving, moving house. I don't want to move, move house. I told Mama but she said we had to move and wouldn't tell me why. Papa... *shouted!* Shouted at me. And said, "We cannot live here anymore!"
I asked him, "Why? Why Papa?" and he *shouted*, shouted again and said it was none of my business! I cried myself to sleep that night.
A week, a week later most of my stuff was gone and the things that were there were packed, packed in boxes.
A week, a week later we were about to leave, I had no idea where we were going. They took me from them, my own parents. My hair was chopped off and they made, made me wear new, new clothes. I did not like my new clothes, I liked my old ones. Mama and Papa were strict on me being clean but not like this!
I met the matron, she was the meanest out of the whole lot. I can't recall everything but, one night I was crying, crying myself to sleep. Then suddenly out of the darkness, he came... "No he, he is dead." Me and him went flying over the skies to Mama and Papa's wings and we bought a new coat. Then we flew to the little cottage by a stream but the little cottage by a stream was not there!

Suddenly I felt I was being sucked into something! A bright light, black, white, *boom!* I was in the workhouse, there was the new coat just... hanging.

Annabel Grace Woods (10)

The Mer-Bear

The Mer-bear is a mixture of a mermaid and a bear. It moves quickly with its scaly tail and lives in the deep seas (but not too deep). It's a nice creature, unless you hurt it. If you do it will whack you in the face with *power!* As well as a tail, the Mer-bear has a furry body and nice, light blue eyes (if not angry) and always has a big smile (most of the time). The Mer-bear is a herbivore so it never eats any types of meat. If they do, they will get very ill. So instead of meat they eat seaweed, coral and more non-meat things from the oceans and seas. But weirdly never honey on its own.

A Mer-bear lives in the middle of an ocean or a sea. "Why the middle?" you may ask. Well, if they go too deep they can't see or find food because they don't have a light. If they are too high up they will burn from the sun because their fur is too fragile for heat. So it's just right for them and their families, from four to six Mer-bears, that go in the middle so they can see but not get burnt.

To finish this, here is some grammar of what to call them:

Age zero to twelve: Mer-let, a mermaid with bear ears.

Age thirteen to nineteen: Bear-maid, starts to have fur.

Age twenty to any age (they can live up to 100): Mer-bear, fully grown and they have got all features.

Fabulous fact one:

The Mer-bear loves to swim and talk and have time with family.

Fabulous fact two:
If you want a Mer-bear friend of your own, follow these steps:
One: get seaweed and cover it with honey.
Two: go to your nearest ocean or sea.
Three: put it on the shore and wait.
Four: when it smells it, it will eat it and be your friend.
PS. If you become its friend, it will give you nice coral decor every day!

Aoife Attwood (10)

The Animal Life

A lpacas chew sideways and are found on a farm in town.
B ats all fly around and hang upside down.
C ats aren't very loyal as they walk around the street.
D ogs give you lots of love, especially for a treat.
E lephants are grey and big and use their trunk to spray.
F rogs jump out of water and take flies as prey.
G iraffes get the high leaves because their necks are long.
H edgehogs use their spikes when scared to make them feel strong.
I guanas like to sunbathe but are good in a fight.
J ellyfish can sting but with no brain, they're never right.
K ittens are baby cats, they're cute and play in the sand.
L ions are vicious but are kings of their land.
M onkeys swing from tree to tree and are super strong.
N ubian goats play for hours and hours long.
O ctopuses squirt dark ink and they have eight legs.
P enguin girls go out and hunt and boys protect the eggs.
Q uickest mammal is a cheetah, they are really fast.
R hinos are super strong and won't let anyone past.
S harks live in water and hunt when they smell blood.
T igers are orange and black and lie in the mud.
U nless you go to the zoo you don't see them all.
V ery often the animals are standing proud and tall.
W olves stay in packs and mainly come out at night.
X -ray tetra is a type of fish which can easily get a fright.

Y es, this poem is very nearly done.
Z ebra is the last animal, I hope you've had fun.

Mia James (8)

A Citizen's Guide To The Mystic Train

A train goes by every morning and night,
At eight o'clock.
Never early, never late.
Give your ticket to the conductor quickly
And be on your way.
It's better to be fast.
If you fumble for your ticket for too long,
The conductor may let you off early as revenge
And trust me.
You don't want to do that.
Remember, if you've selected a certain seat
Go to that seat.
Don't forget it.
You'll need to remember it for the way back.
Well, if you get there at the right time that is.
As for the train ride,
Enjoy the scenery!
My favourite sights are the pink clouds
And the waterfall trees.
If you see eyes looking at you,
Ignore them.
They're purely watching.
They won't harm you as long as you're on the train.

Rumour has it that the eyes belong to those
Who didn't get off at the right stop.
If you see someone covering their face with a newspaper,
Move seats immediately!
It's probably one of the eyeless visitors
Trying to reclaim their eyes.
Make sure you have your train ticket with you.
Hold onto it tightly.
Don't get off too early,
But don't get off too late either.
Only get off at your designated stop!
I recommend getting off at Moonlight Square,
You're unlikely to get lost in the town
And the station is easy to find.
As of which,
Don't get on or off at Haunting Hollow.
The train usually gets a visit from
Some spirits which haunt the nearby butchers.
If you get off at the wrong stop,
Well…
No one actually really knows.
Make sure you don't forget your ticket.
And as always,
Don't forget your watch.
You wouldn't want to miss the train.
Enjoy the ride!

Isla Tully (10)

What Am I?

We come in many different colours, shapes and sizes. Some of us are tall and skinny, while others are big and broad. We display an array of colours and we can be ravishing red or gorgeous green. Some of us carry delicate patterns while others are a singular colour and texture.

Although we don't talk, it does not mean that we don't have feelings. Don't just leave us and expect us to grow. If our habitat is outdoors, come and visit us, care for our environment and appreciate our beauty and we will shine. For those residing indoors, feed them, trim them and change their position so that they have a good balance of sun and shade.

Stop shearing us down! You mangle an estimated forty-one million of some of us every day. This is devastating for you and us. For you, that will mean your oxygen levels are decreasing each and every day. If you continue this practice we will dwindle, and it will change your habitat forever with lasting effects for you and all inhabitants.

So you see, although we do not talk, we have numerous benefits and they will be everlasting. So don't disregard us when you see us, appreciate us, pay us some much-deserved attention so that we may remain here forever and ever. In fact, it is nearly impossible to live without us, not to mention how miserable it would be, the whole environmental cycle would collapse. Not only are we magnificent and beautiful but we have numerous benefits for all, so don't let us fall.

Do you know what I am?

Answer: Trees.

Raeesah Khan (11)

Shall Safety Be My Friend?

Soon safety will be my friend,
Howl, swish, screech.
Soon safety will be my friend.
The wind exhales almighty huffs,
Pressing forcefully against my eyes.
The wind is as dangerous as a fearsome dragon.
I will fight through the uncontrollable, violent wind
With hope pounding in my eyes.

Soon safety will be my friend,
Creak, snap, crack.
Soon safety will be my friend.
The boat bobs up, down, side to side,
Tossing me through the unforgivable waves.
The boat is my only guide, like the loneliest star in the sky.
No matter how suffocating and uncomfortable it gets,
It shall lead me to my only safe destination.

Soon safety will be my friend,
Gush, whip, churn.
Soon safety will be my friend.
The sea is a deafening, monstrous beast.
It spits aggressively, showering me with its saliva.
The sea is like a shambolic bull
Threatening me with its choppy waters.
I will fight my way through the overtaking, swelling sea
With all my courage.

Soon safety will be my friend,
Sizzle, thump, bump.
Soon safety will be my friend.
I land with a boink on the boiling saucepan of sand,
The sand is a merciless soul.
It instantly drags me into the quicksand,
Help, help, help.

My end has come.

Sanvi Patel (10)

What It's Like To Be Me

I live in a world only I can see,
I have dyslexia and ASD.
A magical realm that's only mine,
With changing colours that always shine.

Oh, this is me,
What it's like to be me.
What I can see,
How my world can be.

My mind sees things in a special way,
Colours and shapes blend and play.
It's like a puzzle inside my head,
But sometimes it fills me up with dread.

In the kitchen, a recipe unfolds,
But the words play tricks, hard to hold.
Sieve the egg? That doesn't seem right,
But in my world, words take flight like a kite.

Maths can be a tricky maze,
Where numbers hide and letters wave.
Spelling tests and copying lines,
Feel like a wilderness with secret signs.

Yet in my mind, there's so much more,
A world of wonder, an open door.

My creativity is bright and true,
For I can see what others never do.

So I let the letters dance and play,
And let the colours guide my way.
For in my heart, there is a special light,
That makes my world uniquely bright.

Oh, this is me,
What it's like to be me.
What I can see,
How my world can be.
Oh, this is me!
Who I'm meant to be,
And I'm proud to be *me!*

Katherine O'Dornan (9)

Night Fighter

Engines rumble to life.
Oil van with might.
Smoke chokes out of the radial engine.
Water splashes as it hits the ground with a resounding thud.

Night fighter!
Open fire upon it.
The enemy on our tail.
Bombs dropped.
Flank speed.
We are hit.
Take the confidence of the Luftwaffe.
He is not taking it easy.
Turn sharply.
Shook off the swastika.
Night fighter being torn into shreds by Charly.

German tank!
Open fire.
Tank destroyed!
Second panzer tank!
Call for urgent backup.
"Tanks are on their way," called the driver.
Tanks have arrived.
Enemy tanks to the northeast.
Get in your tanks and follow tank one.
Dump as much ammunition as you can into the German tank.

I watch the Germans scrambling for cover.
Black explosion materialises through the tree.
As the main panzer army comes into view.
But the underground German Panzer IVs are no match for our GMC tank destroyers.
The commanders of ours shout, "Fire!"
The Germans are cut down with only five tanks remaining.

Kevin Kovacs (8)

Gwen's Adventure

Once upon a time, there was a cute little baby bird that lived in a far, far, far away jungle. The little baby bird asked their mum, Florence, if they could have some food at the barbecue shop. Their mother said they could not go because there were predators waiting there. They ate birds, lizards, gazelles, any type of animal you could imagine.

At midnight, the little baby bird crept out of her straw bed and went to the barbecue shop. Then, she was so shocked when she went in. Her body was trembling. She saw tigers roar and killer ants. And then, she got killed and sunk into the depths of the frying pan. And she got eaten by the killer ants.

Beware! Do not go into the far, far jungle.

Joseph Lewin (6)

The Adventures Of My Cat Max

One day, my dad bought a cat,
It was grey and my favourite in fact.
It was all grey with patches of white,
With a black tail and eyes sparkling bright.
I asked my dad, "What should we name it that everyone would like?"
Then my dad replied, "Maybe something like Mike?"
Then I said, "Let's name it Max!"
My dad replied, "Wow! Now let's get the food packs!"
Every day we would play and play,
Not stopping until the end of the day.
I made my cat a swinging toy,
That would leave us in great joy.
My cat Max was always playful,
And he was also sometimes grateful.
Someday, I will meet him again soon,
And someday, I will be over the moon!

Esha Raheel (11)

Sunrise And Sunset

In a world so alive
Clouds breathe to thrive
The sun is mean and very hot
While the clouds are cool
but get bullied a lot by this big blazing sun
No one but the sun is having fun

The sun goes down at the end of the day
That's when everyone cheers hooray
In the dead of the night they are free
No longer afraid of their bully

One day they've had enough
They stood up to their bully, who was acting all tough
So one day the sun got ignored
And the sun soon got bored

Sunrise, sunset
Two completely different things
Sunrise, sunset
Two things no one should be afraid of.

Hussain Atif Lone (10)

Like A Butterfly

Why are you so jealous of my valued beauty?
Are you furious that I walk with courage?
Does my rich, dark skin intimidate you?
Don't you know my ancestors were kings and queens?
Why are you so provoked by my black femininity?
Don't you know my skin is worth more than silver and gold?
You may stomp on me,
But like a butterfly, I will flutter to my success.
Does my intelligence threaten you?
Why are you so bitter?
Is it because I am proud of my skin?
Do you want to see me down, head lowered to the ground,
Shoulders dropped like falling teardrops?
You may stomp on my ego,
But like a butterfly, I will flutter to my success.

Danielle Erikume (11)

The White Door

I woke up in the morning, rolled off my bed and hit my head on the wall. As soon as I hit my head on the wall, I saw a white door... I opened it and I found myself on a rock-hard wooden floor...
I was in a house, everything looked fake like I was in a familiar video game. I knew it was Brookhaven, not a casual place to go on Earth because I saw police, robbers, and cars. It was so loud, people were shouting and I could hear so many different sounds. It didn't feel real. It was so annoying because it was outside my house.
As soon as one of my eyes closed, I saw the exact white door I saw in the beginning. I opened it and I was back on my bed at last.

Harnek Landa (8)

The Moon

The moon has a face like a glowing pearl;
She bathes on sleeping cats' tails whilst they're curled,
On parks and trees and Tokyo's streams,
And crows asleep in the tree it seems.
The scruffling hedgehog and the moving louse,
The yowling greyhound by the door of the house,
The snowy owl that relaxes in bed at noon,
All love to be out by the light of the moon.
But all the things that are precious to the day,
Nestle to sleep to be out of her way;
And wildlife and people close their eyes,
Till up in the morning the sun will awake,
And there will be blue skies.

Imogen Lewis (7)

To Magnificent, Hardworking Parents

Dear hardworking parents,

Thank you very much for taking care of me and sacrificing things just for our family. You have done so much for us. You never treat yourself. Instead, all the money you have goes on us. Why not treat yourself for once?

I admire you because you have done so much for us. I can't think of anyone else to admire except my parents.

Thank you for taking care of me and my brother, and thank you for giving me the best gifts. Even if you give me a small gift it still means love.

Thank you for buying me stuff that I need and for helping me when I need to get things done around the house.

Noella Cobbinah (8)

140 Centimetres Tall

When you turn 140 centimetres tall,
You can really ride it all,
Twists, turns and stomach-churning drops,
So high, that you can see rooftops.

139 centimetres tall,
You really felt so small,
But now you have reached that magic number,
The possibilities are full of wonder.

Rides that flip you many a time,
Coloured red, blue or even lime,
Rides that fill you with excitement or glee,
Really quite magically.

Now that I am 141 centimetres tall,
I really am having a ball,
I am looking forward to what my future holds,
In this roller coaster world, I'll be bold.

Dillon Clarke (10)

My Passion Of Football

I have a passion; my passion is football.
Every day I play with my friends and every day I get better!
I haven't always been good at football, it is something that gets better with practice!
Football just started as a silly game but then I took an interest and started lessons.
Now me and my dad have games at the park, and I love being a goalie!
My dream is to be the next Ronaldo and play for Portugal! Ronaldo is my role model and the person I want to be when I grow up!

Casey O'Rourke (10)

A Day At The Beach

The sound of the seagulls in the air,
We know that we will soon be there.
As we walk upon the soft but irritating sand,
We smell the salty air of the beautiful sea.
As the waves come crashing in,
Isn't it the best time to swim?
The ice cream melts in the sun,
Too bad, so sad, at least we're having fun.
Here we come,
The funfair and arcades are going to be fun.
Our car is full of memories and sand,
Soon we will get back on land.

Levi Pitts (9)

The Overlooker

I watch over war and strife,
I watch over death and life.
I watch over dawn and dusk,
I watch over noon and night.

Sat for the past hundred years,
Not disturbed, nothing dare come near.

I watch over as the plants grow and die,
I watch over the land and the sky,
I watch over the dying of every creature,
Worrying about our planet's near future.

Sat here waiting to be freed,
Yet in no rush, I have no need.

Nancy Rossiter-Pointer (11)

School Time

S chool is really fun!
C ome and enjoy school!
H urry up, we don't want to be late!
O oh! This food is good!
O h, I forgot to mention that you can bring a packed lunch.
L ook, it is playtime!

T he maths here is fun!
I n literacy, we learn about the Great Fire of London!
M eet the teachers, they are really kind.
E njoy the snacks at snack time!

Khadija Azeem (6)

One Thing

It will never be sunny
Or you'll never have money.
You'll never have a phone
Or an ice cream cone.
You'll never get a toy
And you'll never get a day that you will enjoy.
We don't have a sofa so we sit on the floor.
My dad lost his job so we are getting poor.
But you'll soon have to notice that
The only one thing,
The thing that you need is...
My pen and writing!

Miri Fogel (10)

The Spider Monster

Once upon a time, there was a little spider, it loved sweeties. It was best friends with Grace and everyone loved it.
There was a little tiny spider as well and it turned into a baby monster spider and it loved walking out in the night time, finding treasure and gold, and it brought it back to Grace and the other spider.
They all went outside and climbed some trees and went on the swings and then came home and jumped on the bed.

Grace Merle McGuire (4)

My Favourite Place

My favourite place is Paultons Park because it's fun and eye-catching and has lots of amazing rides like carousels and roller coasters. Also, they have themed parts of the park like Jurassic Park, Tornado Springs and Critter Creek which I love and some roller coasters spin you around and some make you go backwards. Sometimes they make me nervous and sometimes they make me laugh so that's why I love Paultons Park so much!

Eva Udy (10)

How To Make The Purrfect Cat!

First, gather food and water.
Stir in a cat toy, cotton wool and
Don't forget to add cuddles.
Season with love and hugs, also leftover lunch.
Add a pinch of cat tower so they can
Meow a little louder.
Pour in some dreams of freedom so they can
Wonder about the loyalty
And don't forget the power of positivity
And the wonders of friendship.
Finally, blend some sugar with some joy.

Louise Lin (11)

This Is Me

This is me
A Year Six boy
A mind full of curiosity
And a great big smile
I'll face all the challenges that come my way
I may be lazy but still listen
I'll always take part.

This is me
A Year Six boy
A mind full of curiosity
And a great big smile
I'll face the wonders that come my way
Adventurous, kind, amazing
Name anything, that will be me!

Muhammad Hunnain Ali Shah (11)

Turkey Travels

I went to Turkey and it was astonishing. An ice cream man was snatching the ice cream from me and it was hilarious! I even went to the wonderful ocean. I was very joyful that I couldn't resist it. The atmosphere was really amazing. Oh yeah, the best part was the delightful, scrumptious food! Also, there were so many attraction places to visit.
This is my holiday story and I had a great time!

Amyra Qoudos (8)

The Journey

The boat was a massive mountain
Crashing against the swishing sea.
High in the sky, birds flew past,
Waving goodbye.
Jamaica
Jamaica
Jamaica.

The wind blew against me.
The sky frowned down.
But as the band played
I laughed and laughed.
Jamaica
Jamaica
Jamaica.

Watching
Everyone
Wave
Goodbye.

Emily Rose Hopewell (8)

Nightmare

N ightmare, here you come
I n my dreams you overtake
G iven powers to bring sadness to my eyes
H ere you are occurring now
T o my peak until I scream
M y lord, you freak me out
A nd perish as it is real
R aging as daylight approaches then you vanish
E arly in the morning, I wake up from dread.

Stuti Shah (10)

Grinch

He's mean, he's green
And he has teeth that are unclean.
He's grouchy, he's greedy,
He's sneaky, he's selfish.
Just one lonely soul,
With one stubborn cold heart.
He's bad, he's mad
With a round belly
And a heart two sizes small.
That's why he hates Christmas
With its joy and snowfall.

Ali Abdullah (9)

Empty Evenings

The night is cold,
The moon a shiny star,
I can see the afraid eyes but only from afar,
The trees are a dark green,
But no bright flowers to be seen,
The TV empty just like me,
But I don't want to be,
I just want to be free,
"Dear God," I plead,
"How can I proceed?"
Though I bleed,
I hope you don't end up like me...

Annalisa Burton (12)

Animals

My doggy says woof woof woof
And wags their tail.
She goes in the water and digs holes.

Monkeys go ooh ooh aah aah
And swing in trees.
They play with their friends.

Horses make a neigh neigh sound
And I like three of them.
They are big so people sit on them.

Harmony James (4)

Summer's Football Dreams!

I put my boots on ready to play
In a stadium far, far away.
The fans are singing our song
Because they know I like to play along.
Scoring a goal is oh-so-fun
Although some haters stick out a tongue.
As I await the whistle to blow
I just go along with the flow.

Summer Grainger (10)

My First Pond Visit

One day, during the holiday. My daddy promised to take my sister and me to the pond. On that Saturday, he took my sister and me out of the house and we walked down the street to see the pond. I saw a lot of ducks and fishes. I was so happy and made my daddy promise to bring us there again.

Ozichukwu Egbeogu (5)

Teachers

T each us.
E xplain work.
A lways fair.
C ool geography lessons.
H elp us with work.
E xplain work.
R eally interesting lessons.
S uper nice stories.

Kerem Dogan (7)

The Ocean

The turquoise waves crash
A beautiful blue blanket
Shimmers in the sun
White, turquoise and blue ribbons
Silhouettes swim underneath
The ocean is still until
Some whales break the surface.

Josie Pollard (10)

Nature

Leaves falling one by one,
The beauty hides behind,
Every season, every day,
No nature goes away,
No creature scares you away,
Because Mother Nature is by your side.

Thananiya Thevakanthan (9)

Eshaal

E nergetic and expert in English
S miley and smart
H appy and helpful
A mazing and acrobatic
A lways kind
L oving.

Eshaal Fatima Shah

My Body Moves

My legs run and walk.
My hands write and clap.
My mouth talks and sings.
My eyes blink and look.
My feet stamp and tiptoe.
My ears hear and wiggle.

Aanya Kaul (5)

Worship

Dear Sir/Madam,
I want to be a worship leader because I go to church every week, I'm in the church choir and I go to worship for all. I will have good ideas!

Spencer Brookes (11)

Young Writers Information

We hope you have enjoyed reading this book – and that you will continue to in the coming years.

If you're a young writer who enjoys reading and creative writing, or the parent of an enthusiastic poet or story writer, do visit our website **www.youngwriters.co.uk**. Here you will find free competitions, workshops and games, as well as recommended reads, a poetry glossary and our blog. There's lots to keep budding writers motivated to write!

If you would like to order further copies of this book, or any of our other titles, then please give us a call or order via your online account.

Young Writers
Remus House
Coltsfoot Drive
Peterborough
PE2 9BF
(01733) 890066
info@youngwriters.co.uk

Join in the conversation!
Tips, news, giveaways and much more!

YoungWritersUK   YoungWritersCW
youngwriterscw   youngwriterscw